Sunset

Spas, Hot Tubs & Home Saunas

By the Editors of Sunset Books
and Sunset Magazine

Lane Publishing Co. ■ **Menlo Park, California**

Research & Text
Susan Warton
Paul Spring

Coordinating Editor
Cornelia Fogle

Design
Joe di Chiarro

Illustrations
Rik Olson
Terrence Meagher

Photography: Ed Bigelow: 35, 37 top, 45 right. Glenn Christiansen: 54 bottom. Stephen Marley: 33, 36, 38, 40, 41, 42, 45 left, 47, 53, 55, 63, 64. Ells Marugg: 44, 51 top. John McCarthy: 61 top. Jack McDowell: 34, 37 bottom, 39, 43, 46, 48, 49, 50, 52, 56, 57, 58, 59, 60 bottom, 61 bottom, 62. Jim Peck: 51 bottom. Norm Plate: 60 top. Darrow M. Watt: 54 top.

Cover: Bounded by a large, free-form koi pond lined with ferns and natural boulders, this tiled in-ground spa is still only steps away from the house. (For more on this spa, see page 47.) Spa design by Pacific Water Works and Rob Newman. Cover design by Roger Flanagan. Photograph by Stephen Marley.

Sunset Books
Editor: David E. Clark
Managing Editor: Elizabeth L. Hogan

First printing October 1986

 Library of Congress Catalog Card Number: 86-80871. ISBN 0-376-01247-1. Lithographed in the United States.

Hot News

Heat—whether wet, as in a spa or hot tub, or dry, as in a sauna—has long been a popular way of relaxing body and mind. After work or a workout, a bubbly spa or hot tub releases tensions through gentle hydromassage. Finland's famous sauna works the same wonders with soothing dry heat. It's all explained here, with full details on location and landscaping, equipment, and maintenance.

For their careful review of the manuscript and their generosity with their expertise, we extend special thanks to Stephen Blum of Leisure Time Chemical Corporation, Irwindale, California, and the International Spa and Hot Tub Council of the National Spa and Pool Institute, Alexandria, Virginia; Alan Kallerman and Chet Lockwood of Neptune Pool & Spa, Palo Alto, California; John Kolkka of Finnish-American Sauna Company, Redwood City, California; Jim McNicol of Brett Aqualine, Inc., Huntington Beach, California; and Tom Neal of Watkins Manufacturing Corporation, Carlsbad, California.

We are also grateful to Creative Contracting of Novato, California; Creative Energy of San Rafael, California; Pat Ewing and Judy Ramminger of the National Spa and Pool Institute, Alexandria, Virginia; Jeff Farber of Hot Water World, Mill Valley, California; Jim Henderson of New Products, Inc., Novato, California; Lance Kegler of East Bay Builders, Fremont, California; John Kilroy of Hot Water Living Magazine, Irvine, California; Susan Kopicki of Spa and Sauna Journal, Irvine, California; Charles Lemmonier of Gazebo Nostalgia, Walnut Creek, California; and Lynda Sisk of Pacific Water Works, Santa Cruz, California.

Finally, we extend special thanks to Fran Feldman for copyediting the manuscript, and to JoAnn Masaoka for styling some of the photographs.

Contents

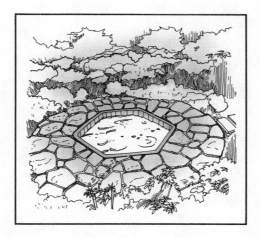

A Spa & Hot Tub Primer

- **Portable spas**
- **In-ground spas**
- **Hot tubs**
- **Support equipment**
- **Landscaping ideas**
- **Maintenance**

Throughout history, people of both eastern and western societies have soaked their cares away in hot baths. Today, Americans are rediscovering this age-old pleasure.

The appeal could not be more obvious. Hot hydromassage can soothe away tensions and stress in a matter of minutes. Whether taken as a morning ritual or after a grueling day at the office, a hot soak in a spa or hot tub gently replenishes body and mind as no other tonic can. What's more, hydrotherapy is absolutely harmless—even wholesome—for almost everyone. What doctors and athletes have known for a long time is fast becoming a splashy new trend for the rest of us.

If you're thinking of getting into hot water yourself, this chapter will introduce you to this fascinating subject. From landscaping ideas to maintenance details, it covers every aspect of the home spa and hot tub and will help you design an installation of your own.

Old woodcut *proves that tubs are not a new idea at all.*

Spas and hot tubs have enjoyed increasing popularity among many Americans in recent years. Even if you don't own one, chances are you've experienced a pleasurable soak in a friend's spa or tub or in the spa at a hotel or resort area.

If you live in an apartment complex, you know that its hot, bubbly spa is as basic and well-used a feature as the laundry room. Or perhaps you've enjoyed a hot, jetted soak in one of today's spalike bathtubs, another phenomenon of the hot water craze, or in the motionless, extra-hot water of the traditional Japanese *ofuro* (see page 54 for an example).

The hot water experience we describe in this chapter relates exclusively to the most popular forms—the spa and hot tub. To soak in either of these is not really to take a bath. Ideally, you enter the water when freshly clean from a shower. You never use soap and you generally take soaks outdoors or in a special spa/tub room, rather than in the bathroom. Though of course it is possible to drain a spa or hot tub, you do this infrequently, not after each soak. Instead, a filter and a sanitizing agent, such as chlorine, keep the spa or tub water clean and maintain it in a sparkling clear condition. The system is similar to that of a swimming pool but has little in common with an ordinary bathtub.

Hot Hydrohistory

Though many ancient cultures—
Roman, Egyptian, Greek, Turkish,
and Japanese—enjoyed some form of communal hot bathing, the modern hot tub and spa can be most easily traced to Roman and Japanese predecessors.

Ancient Roman baths had less to do with personal hygiene than with conviviality. Large, often boisterous aquatic arenas, these baths could accommodate thousands of people at once. Here, a Roman went to soak in the hot waters, to relax, and to socialize with friends.

For centuries, the Japanese have enjoyed the pleasure of hot bathing in the freestanding wooden *ofuro*. Unlike the crowded Roman experience, hot bathing in Japan has often been a private, family affair.

Though modern Americans are better known for their quick morning showers, hot water bathing has also been commonplace in American culture. Following the fashion of great European resort spas, American resorts such as Saratoga Springs in New York, Warm Springs in Georgia, and Calistoga in California have long attracted wealthy patrons to their hot, therapeutic mineral waters.

California Ingenuity

It was left to a group of Californians to combine the conviviality of the Roman bath, the tranquility of the Japanese ofuro, and the therapeutic quality of hot mineral springs into prototypes of today's spas and hot tubs.

At the turn of the century, Santa Barbara was a mecca for the social elite, who partook of its nearby canyon hot springs. In the late 1960s, though the springs had long since slipped in status, a creative handful of Santa Barbarans decided to bring the pleasures of hot bathing from the canyons into their own back yards. Some of them had tried the Japanese ofuro, as well, and found the experience too delightful not to repeat.

As if to dispel the myth that hot soaking had to be a sport of the rich, they built their back-yard baths of salvage materials—wine vats, water tanks, sidearm heaters, and pieces of pipe. With the addition of makeshift pumps, the first hot tubs were born.

Meanwhile, in nearby Los Angeles, many pool contractors already knew how to build good spas, but only by a very tedious method. In those days, gunite, a mixture of sand and cement blown through a special gun, was used to make the spas that often adjoined swimming pools at the homes of the well-to-do of Hollywood. But gunite was—and still is— costly, as well as difficult to use. Technology gradually overcame the inconvenience of gunite and other concrete methods, leading to the creation of a lightweight, molded spa shell. From this innovation evolved today's thermoplastic spas, with their great variety of shapes, sizes, and colors.

Spa or Tub— Which Is for You?

The early molded spas have given way to acrylic and even newer thermoplastic spas that present consumers with a dizzying array of shapes, sizes, colors, and luxurious options. Likewise, since the days of wine-barrel bathing in California in the late 1960s, a small but sophisticated cooperage industry producing sleek, jetted wood tubs has evolved.

All this has happened very fast. As a result, many people still aren't clear on how a spa differs from a hot tub.

Both a spa and a tub massage bathers with a froth of hot, moving water. Tiny, bursting bubbles add to the experience. Moreover, support equipment for spas and tubs is virtually identical. Even the popular expression "hot-tubbing" can refer to soaking in either kind of vessel.

Still, there are important differences between the two that lead consumers toward a preference for one over the other. For many, the choice is almost automatic because one or the other fits the family better. Before you decide, look carefully at some of the differences discussed below.

Paradise in Plastic

Today's sleek, contemporary spa departs completely from the rustic simplicity of hot tub design and manufacture. The choices in spas are dazzling, running the gamut from boxy little portables to tiled and landscaped installations of splendid proportions.

Spas fall into two general categories—in-ground and portable. The first, the older and more traditional type, is sunken in the ground or placed in a deck, and is usually installed by a contractor. The portable, or self-contained, spa is more like a home appliance: it doesn't have to be permanently installed and comes as a complete unit, ready to plug into a 110-volt outlet or wired to a 220-volt circuit. Its support equipment—and every other necessity except water—come as part of the package. Such spas are manufactured by a number of companies, both large and small. (For information on purchasing a spa, see page 20.)

Most spas have a plastic surface, either acrylic (bonded to fiberglass) or

one of the newer and more durable plastics. Some in-ground spas are finished with tile. Though a spa's slick surface may be easier to keep scrupulously clean than the porous wood of some hot tubs, good maintenance is essential. Any spa can become very troublesome if proper care is neglected.

For a closer look at all types of spas, read the section "Today's Spa: A New Wave of Choices," below. A colorful display of indoor and outdoor spa designs begins on page 33. Many more exciting possibilities await you in dealers' showrooms.

The Natural Way

Soft and rustic, hot tubs derive their appeal from their smooth wood surfaces. One of the most common statements of tub-lovers is that the wood surrounding their soak feels good to touch. For them it conveys a warmth and comfort that enhances the soothing, meditative experience of soaking. They also like its pleasant, musty aroma.

Whether made of redwood, cedar, teak, or another wood, hot tubs also boast a classic beauty. And no wonder: the tub's simple lines reflect barrel design that has remained unchanged for centuries.

With a greater gallonage capacity than most spas, hot tubs give a deep soak, which some people prefer. A tub that's 4 or 5 feet deep can immerse you up to your neck, thanks in part to more spartan seating options compared to the body-conforming contours of some shallow spa seats. Tubs also allow more choice in number and placement of hydrojets.

For all the natural luxury of wood, however, some hot tubs have given their owners problems after a few years, mainly due to neglect. Careful maintenance of a hot tub, as explained in the section beginning on page 30, is essential to its longevity. Anything less can result in irreparable damage.

If the tub is drained and allowed to dry for more than 2 days, leaks can develop between the staves when the tub is refilled. This is because stave edges will no longer swell evenly to create a continuous seal.

If you allow the water chemistry to go awry, excessive chlorine or bromine can begin to break down the wood. Conversely, not enough will allow harmful bacteria to lodge in the wood's porous surface, creating the danger of infection for bathers. Because of its depth, draining and scrubbing a hot tub also demands a little extra effort.

If the wood tub attracts you but you don't want the extra work, investigate the "spa-tubs." On the outside, these hybrid creations are like any other hot tub; but inside, they're fitted with a smooth, plastic liner, just like any spa.

For details on the traditional hot tub, turn to page 12. Photographed in color, hot tubs appear in many settings in the chapter beginning on page 33.

Today's Spa: A New Wave of Choices

Just a few years ago, it was better known as the whirlpool bath, which most people thought of as a medically prescribed remedy for ailing muscles. Known today as the spa, it has obviously become something much bigger and splashier.

While hot hydromassage remains as therapeutic to muscles as before, its role in today's spa is regarded more as an enhancement than as a medicinal cure. People now appreciate the spa simply because hydrotherapy feels so good. And when you add to it the conviviality of a hot soak

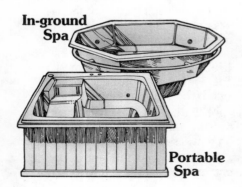

In-ground Spa

Portable Spa

Hot Tub

with a few friends, the experience becomes even more pleasurable.

When water is heated, it works as a relaxing tonic. The 100° to 104°F/ 38° to 40°C temperature of spa or tub water dilates blood vessels, slows down the pulse, and slightly enlarges the heart, allowing it to work 10 to 20 percent more efficiently. As circulation improves throughout the body, muscles are soothed.

Thus, it should come as no surprise that a booming young industry is springing up to satisfy the demand for home spas. The drawings on pages 8 and 9 only hint at the many styles, shapes, and sizes now available. Shopping for a spa will remind you of shopping for a new car. You'll see a similar panorama of gleaming styles and colors, along with almost as much sophistication in basic and optional equipment. As for cost, cars generally carry higher price tags, although the price differential between a luxury spa and an economy car may not be much.

Your basic choice of spa lies between the portable, or self-contained, type and the in-ground spa shell with separate support equipment. Portable possibilities are discussed below. For information on the in-ground spa, see page 9.

Portable Spas

Newest splash in the hot water industry, the portable spa probably took shape in answer to the impermanence of today's life-style. Because the portable spa sits above ground, it requires nothing more than a slab underneath. A "skirt," typically made of redwood, surrounds the shell.

Unlike the in-ground spa and the hot tub, a portable spa is truly self-contained: its support equipment is hidden by the skirt, close beside the lightweight plastic shell. These spas typically are heated by electricity; 110-volt models are designed to be taken home and plugged into an outlet. In this way, set-up time and expense is minimized.

Hot Water Safety

To hot water devotees, soaking in a bubbling spa or tub provides one of life's supreme pleasures. But, to ensure that the experience is a safe, healthy one requires taking responsibility for basic safety, as well as using a little common sense. For a few people, this may mean not soaking in a spa or hot tub at all.

■ People with heart disease, diabetes, high or low blood pressure, or any serious illness should not enter a spa or hot tub without first consulting their physician.

■ Pregnant women should also stay out of a spa or hot tub unless their physician has advised them it's safe.

■ Soaking for too long in high water temperatures can elevate anyone's body heat beyond safe limits. The National Spa and Pool Institute considers 104°F/40°C to be the maximum safe water temperature for adults, with a safe soaking time of no longer than 15 minutes. Some medical authorities think that the maximum safe temperature should be lower—100° to 102°F/ 38° to 39°C. For infants and children, who are especially sensitive to heat, the temperature should be no higher than 95°F/35°C, with a safe soaking time of no longer than 10 minutes. Introduce the child slowly to the water to be sure there's no fear or discomfort.

■ Even a shallow spa or tub contains enough water to drown a bather. Never let children soak without adult supervision. It is also unwise for an adult to soak alone.

Do not allow jumping, diving, or underwater swimming. Long hair can be pulled into uncovered drains by strong suction, then become tangled. Keep grates and drain covers in good repair and secured in place, and make sure that bathers stay away from these outlets (on the spa floor).

■ No one who has an external infection or wound should get into a spa or hot tub, since hot water easily carries the infection to others. Also, do not enter the water unless it has been properly tested and sanitized (see page 30), and its temperature checked with an accurate thermometer.

■ Alcohol and drugs don't mix safely with use of a spa or hot tub. The hot water intensifies their effect, sometimes dangerously. Avoid their use both prior to and during a soak. Instead, enjoy chilled juice or mineral water while soaking.

■ NEVER handle a telephone or electrical appliance when you are in the water or when your hands are wet. The building code restriction that any spa or tub must stand at least 5 feet from any electrical outlet is intended to prevent a TV, radio, or other electrical device from being placed on the spa edge. Should any such appliance fall into the water, it could electrocute the bathers.

■ Keep the spa or tub securely covered when not in use. If the cover doesn't lock or batten down securely, make sure there is also childproof fencing to keep curious children and animals out. Always remove the cover completely before entering the water.

■ Use common sense to prevent accidents. Provide skidproof surfaces around the spa or hot tub. Serve food and drinks in plastic containers to avoid the danger of broken glass. Provide adequate lighting, near ground level, at steps, and other hazardous spots.

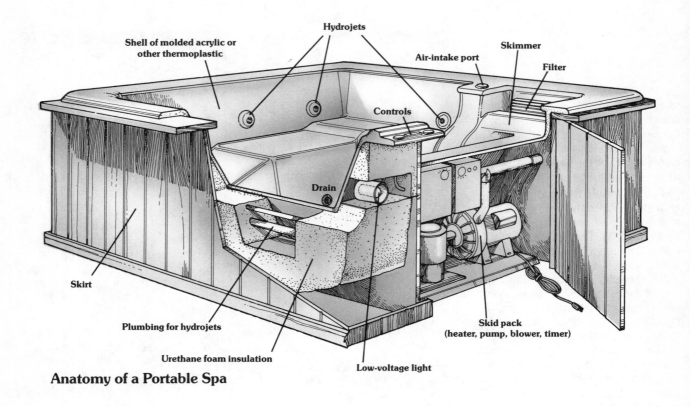

Hydrojets

Shell of molded acrylic or
other thermoplastic

Air-intake port

Skimmer

Filter

Controls

Drain

Skirt

Plumbing for hydrojets

Urethane foam insulation

Low-voltage light

Skid pack
(heater, pump, blower, timer)

Anatomy of a Portable Spa

Sizing Up the Benefits

Because most portable spas are relatively shallow, with a water depth of between 26 and 36 inches, you can stand them on their sides to move them through a standard doorway. With a dry average weight of 300 to 500 pounds, a portable can be lifted with enough manpower. More accurately classified as a large home appliance than a permanent home improvement, the portable spa can be moved from one setting to another—for example, from a deck into a sunroom, or from your old to your new home.

Portables typically range in size from a 4- by 5-foot spa that holds about 125 gallons to an 8-foot one that contains 500 gallons. The smallest seats two; the largest can accommodate up to eight.

Keep in mind, however, that many portables are relatively shallow; this shallow depth is compensated for by special, often reclining, seats. But if you want a truly deep soak, look for portables with deep seating, or turn to an in-ground spa or a hot tub.

Ask your dealer if it's possible to try out the portable spa you're consid-

ering. If it's filled with hot water, you'll be able to tell just how comfortable the seats, hydrojets, and other important variables are before you purchase.

Operating the Spa

Another unique feature of the portable spa is that all its support equipment—heater, filter, pump, air blower, and hydrojets—is contained in its skirt. A small door in one side

makes the equipment accessible for maintenance or repair.

Like the shell itself, the portable's equipment is a smaller version of what would be necessary to support a large, in-ground spa or hot tub, resulting in less power and capacity. Each piece of equipment is, however, matched to the relatively small water volume of the portable, so the spa functions more economically than a spa or tub with larger equipment and more water to heat.

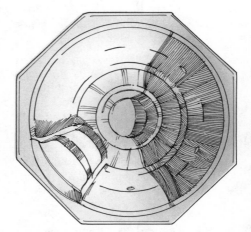
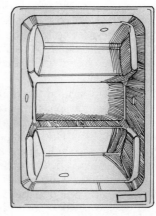

Freedom of form characterizes spas, both portable and in-ground. Presented here are

Many portable spas run on 110 volts. But before you bring one home, be sure to check out your home's electrical system. If you have any doubt about a circuit's capacity to take a 110-volt portable spa, have it checked out by a licensed electrician.

The outlet you use for the spa must be part of a 20-amp circuit that doesn't service any other heavy-draw appliances. Nearly all portables are now internally wired with ground fault circuit interrupters (GFCI); if not, your outlet or its circuit must have such protection.

Another option offered by many spa manufacturers is to run the equipment on 220 volts, accomplished by adding a new circuit and hard-wiring the spa directly to it. You will have to hire a licensed electrician or spa contractor for this job. Although the spa will no longer be as portable, you'll gain considerable heating speed. Also, with 220 volts you can run the heater simultaneously with the hydrojets and blower for a long period of time—not possible with a 110-volt heater.

If your spa is less than fully insulated, a 220-volt, 6kw heater is a real advantage. It will raise water temperature much faster than a small 110-volt, 1.5kw heater, so you'll have a shorter wait before you can enter the spa; it also means that the spa can maintain a steady temperature of 100° to 104°F/38° to 40°C, even if you're in and out of the water. A smaller heater can have

trouble keeping up with the heat loss. (Air blowers, as explained on page 17, also cool down the water quickly.)

Gas heaters, or gas packs, for portable spas are also available; the newer units no longer require remote installation. However, with gas your portable will no longer be self-contained. For more information on heaters, turn to page 16.

Other Considerations

Besides mobility, the other advantage to the portable spa is its relatively low cost. An excellent portable can be purchased for substantially less than an in-ground spa.

Since it's a self-contained appliance rather than a property improvement, the portable spa usually requires no building permit (check with your local building department to be sure); nor will it raise your property taxes. And you won't have to endure weeks—or even months—of construction before you can enjoy your first hot soak.

The In-ground Spa

Before the portable appeared on the market, the only spa available was what the industry now calls in-ground. As the name implies, these

spas (the earliest were made of poured concrete or concrete block) were placed in a hole dug in the ground. Today, the term also refers to spas set into an above-grade surface, such as a deck.

The support equipment necessary for an in-ground spa always stands a short distance away, in its own housing. Although this requires more planning and construction, it also allows you more choice on types and sizes of equipment.

Shopping for an in-ground spa means choosing between a factory-molded shell (probably made of fiberglass-reinforced acrylic or one of the newer plastics that doesn't require a fiberglass backing) and the more expensive, longer-lasting shell made of concrete. Each type offers myriad shapes and sizes from which to choose.

If you decide on the manufactured shell, by far the most popular, you can buy the entire package—including equipment and installation—from a full-service dealer, one who is licensed to both sell and install the spa. An alternative is to buy a ready-made spa and the necessary support equipment from a reputable dealer, then hire a contractor recommended by the dealer to install it.

If you choose concrete, the spa will be formed on site by a pool contractor. Most pool companies provide a design service, but if a spa is only one element of an entire backyard redesign, consider hiring a landscape architect to handle everything.

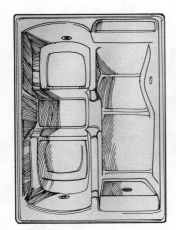 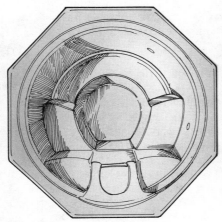 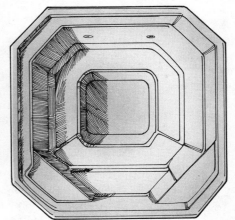

five of the choices currently available in dealers' showrooms.

Whether the shell is made of plastic or concrete, an in-ground spa installation requires tearing up the garden—or deck—to some extent. Plumbing and wiring lines need to be buried or hidden, and support equipment has to be sheltered. Often, the shell is fully or partially recessed into an excavation.

For these reasons, installing an in-ground spa involves a lot more than simply purchasing an off-the-shelf portable. Though usually longer lasting and more attractively landscaped, the in-ground spa also means more planning, disruption, cost, and time.

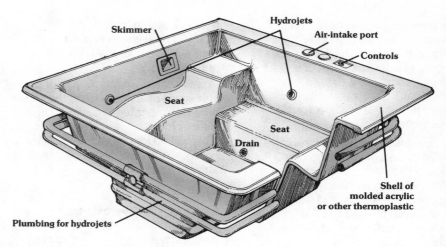

Anatomy of an In-ground Spa

Concrete, the Earliest Spas

Offshoots of the swimming pool industry, the earliest home spas were built, like pools, of concrete. Today, when the concrete method is used for a new spa, in many cases a swimming pool is also under construction, and the two will share the support equipment.

The first concrete methods used—construction by concrete blocks or poured concrete—were poorly suited to freeform spas. It was difficult to create curves, and corners tended to trap dirt.

A more streamlined concrete method, gunite, eventually resolved the shaping difficulty. In the gunite method, a mesh of reinforcement rods forms the curved spa shape inside the excavation. Gunite, an almost dry sand-and-cement mixture, is drawn from a transit mixer and

shot under high pressure through a nozzle onto the reinforcement. Because the reinforcing mesh is flexible, gunite spas can be custom designed to take on attractive, sculptural shapes, an advantage over their molded plastic counterparts.

Perhaps because they're familiar with swimming pool construction, landscape architects often favor concrete spas over plastic alternatives. Also, concrete lasts at least a lifetime. But because they require specialized equipment and expert skill, all concrete methods are costly. Nevertheless, using concrete for a spa is justified, especially in situations where a concrete pool is also being installed.

All of the concrete methods result in a rough-textured surface, often coated with smooth plaster. Replastering becomes necessary about every 5 to 7 years. A gleaming tile finish can enhance the spa's appearance.

Plastic In-ground Spas

The majority of today's in-ground spas are made of acrylic reinforced with fiberglass, although an increasing number are being manufactured from high-impact plastics. Gelcoat is rarely used any longer, but many older spas are made of this material. For a more complete discussion of spa shell materials, see the opposite page.

Tile, fastened with a special adhesive, can be used to cover any of the shells mentioned above. This can be done on site or, more typically, as part of the manufacturing process.

Unlike gunite and other concrete spas which are formed inside the hollow excavated for them, a plastic spa shell is molded in a factory. Delivered to the site, it is lowered into position—usually in an excavation or deck opening. A spa placed in the ground must be supported on the bottom and sides with sand. An aboveground shell is supported by a concrete slab and by heavy wood framing.

Though lower in cost than a concrete spa, the plastic in-ground type is more expensive than most portables, but it is likely to last longer.

In-ground Spa Installation

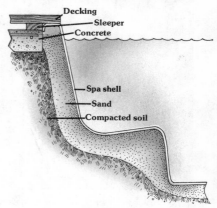

Concrete Spa Installation

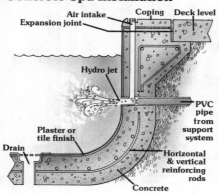

Swim Spa

The Swim Spa

Many of today's fitness buffs look forward to a relaxing hot soak after cooling down from a strenuous workout. Recently, a fascinating offshoot of the spa industry has surfaced which allows them to do both. It's called the swim spa. A typical example (*see above*) looks like an elongated version of any other in-ground spa.

In the cooler swim spa, swirling white water is propelled by two or more strong hydrojets. Without moving forward an inch, a swimmer can cover miles, simply by swimming against this raging current.

For a hot soak, the thermostat can be turned up, or in some models, a barrier can be dropped in place across the width of the pool that will create a typical hot, jetted spa at one end separate from the more tepid water and its powerful jets at the other.

Working with Installation Professionals

The spa industry is still relatively new and growing fast. Under the circumstances, it pays to take extra precautions, not only in selecting materials but also in choosing a contractor.

Contractors. If you buy your spa from a full service dealer, this greatly simplifies the installation. As part

of your package, the dealer, who is often a licensed general or specialty contractor, will do all the work needed to install the spa and its equipment on your property. (Follow the guidelines on page 20 for choosing a reliable spa dealer.)

If you buy the spa from a dealer who is not licensed to offer you installation service, ask the dealer to recommend a contractor. Of course, you can choose your own, too.

As explained earlier, a concrete installation requires specialized skill and equipment, generally supplied by swimming pool contractors.

Before hiring any professional or making any purchase, be sure to ask for references so you can see some of the person's work and talk to former clients. And check to be sure that the contractor is bonded and insured for workers' compensation.

If the spa is to be installed as part of a broader construction or landscaping job, you may want to start with an architect, designer, or landscape architect.

The contract. It's always important to have a detailed, complete contract that both you and your contractor have agreed on, even if your contractor is also your spa dealer. It should include all the work your contractor will do. Service after the installation should be written up in a separate contract. (Full-service spa

retailers sometimes offer service contracts for spas; so do traditional pool maintenance companies.)

A good contract should include the following items:

• *A completion date.*

• *A complete listing of equipment and services.* The list of equipment should include names of manufacturers and model numbers of all major elements, and general specifications of size and quality for plumbing and electrical components. The list of services should specify who is to perform each part of the work and should show a firm estimate on price for each aspect.

• *All guarantees and warranties.* These must include work guarantees or warranties and equipment guarantees. Manufacturers' guarantees should be appended along with those of the seller and installing contractor. Lengths of all guarantees should be specified. Work guarantees should specify on-site service.

• *Terms of delivery.*

• *Payment schedule.* An ideal contract would provide for payment in no less than three stages: down payment, completion payment, and final payment at the end of any lien period.

Spa Shells

What set off the new wave of spa popularity was the first shell, or water container, made of molded fiberglass, a technology borrowed from fiberglass boat making. Before this innovation, each spa was built on site from poured concrete, concrete blocks, or gunite. These methods, although difficult, time-consuming, and costly, are still used for building swimming pools and the most luxurious spas.

Today, fiberglass is being used mainly as a backing for acrylic spas. It is sprayed onto the back of the vacuum-formed plastic once it has cooled. Some newer plastics on the market don't use fiberglass at all in spa construction.

Fiberglass and Gelcoat

Lightweight, low cost, and easily mass-produced in pleasing, one-piece shapes, the early fiberglass shells were carried to a site and professionally installed. But fiberglass was only the beginning; it needed a lining.

The earliest standard lining for fiberglass, whether used in a spa, boat, or pool, was gelcoat. A polymer resin, gelcoat was sprayed onto the spa shell mold. When hardened, the gelcoat was removed from the mold and sprayed with fiberglass to give it strength.

Problems occurred with gelcoat, however, due to faulty manufacturing or the normal wear and tear of several years' use. High temperatures (over 104°F/40°C) caused the surface to blister, as trapped air bubbles expanded. Colors tended to fade over time, unless protected by periodic waxing with a special product. Finally, delamination resulted when highly chlorinated water seeped through the semiporous gelcoat lining.

Acrylic Spas

Gelcoat's imperfections inevitably led to the use of improved materials, products from today's sophisticated world of plastics.

Many spa shells are now made from acrylic. Dense, nonporous, and as glossy as porcelain, acrylic comes in a riot of colors—from earth tones to vivid primaries, in solids and simulated marbling.

But for all its bright promise, acrylic hasn't always given long-term satisfaction in spas. Over time, it tends to nick and scratch, as well as fade. (The marbled coloration serves more than a decorative purpose: it also camouflages blemishes.)

An important index to long-lasting quality is the thickness of the acrylic sheet prior to molding. In portables, sheets for many spas are ⅛ inch thick; the best spas, however, have linings ³⁄₁₆ inch thick. To make a shell, the acrylic sheet is heated until pliable, then vacuum-pulled into a mold. As it stretches around corners,

an ⅛-inch-thick sheet can become quite thin and susceptible to damage later on.

Another inherent weakness with acrylic shows up after faulty manufacturing. Not strong enough to stand on its own, acrylic requires reinforcement with fiberglass. After cooling and removal from the mold, the acrylic is sprayed underneath with fiberglass. If anything goes wrong during this tricky process—such as the formation of air bubbles—it can lead to delamination of the two materials later on. Extremely high water temperatures or just ordinary wear-and-tear over the years have also caused delamination in some acrylic spas.

New Thermoplastics

These mishaps with acrylic have challenged the plastics industry to adopt even tougher products for spa shells. These plastics are impressive for their sturdiness under adverse conditions and for their high resilience against impact. They're also resistant to damage from sun, chemicals, and temperature extremes, elements which have worn down spas in the past. A few manufacturers use ABS plastic (commonly used for plastic plumbing pipe) or cross-link polyethylene, but the most widely used are ABS-like plastics such as ROVEL® weatherable polymer. These plastics won't discolor, chip, blister, or peel.

Thicker and more resilient than acrylic, these materials, which are co-extruded with an ABS backing, can stand on their own and require no fiberglass reinforcement. To mold the shell, the plastic with its backing is vacuum-formed by the same technique and equipment used for acrylic. Obviously, this eliminates the problem of delamination.

Once limited to only one neutral color, the product now comes in a wide range of solid colors and simulated marbling. Finishes vary from the original leathery texture to new, satin-smooth surfaces. Careful attention has been given to choosing colors that won't fade with exposure to sunlight or chemicals, a problem with the first of these plastics.

The Hot Tub

Although the high tide of their popularity in the 1970s has since ebbed, hot tubs remain the first choice today of people who appreciate the natural beauty of wood and its harmony with garden plants and trees. Tubs are also the choice of those who want a deep soak, along with flexibility in the number and placement of hydrojets. And, for traditionalists, the wooden tub stands unrivalled for its timelessness.

In its heyday, the hot tub sprang up everywhere—at least in the West. Hundreds of thousands were built, some without sufficient care, to meet the demand. Many of these tubs have since deteriorated—some simply due to age, some due to poor craftsmanship, and still others due to construction from inferior materials. But one common reason for their failure has been lack of adequate maintenance.

Hot tubs, like spas, demand a regular maintenance program, as explained on page 30. Water chemistry must be carefully controlled, and the tub must be cleaned periodically. But because tubs are made of organic material—some type of wood—problems can arise with hot tubs that spa owners never encounter. For example, a spa that has been drained and abandoned for a time can usually be renewed. But a tub that is drained and allowed to dry out may never be usable again. The dried wood staves twist and cup, distorting the fit of the original coopering.

You *will* need to empty the tub every few months (see pages 32), but never leave the tub unfilled for more than 2 days.

Which Wood?

Sleek staves of wood, forming the watertight curves of a hot tub, are the essence of its beauty. Wood, with its comforting touch and pleasantly musky fragrance, enhances the appeal of a soak, too.

The kind of wood used for a tub depends primarily on regional availability. Most tubs are made from softwoods; redwood and cedar are the most common, but cypress is also used. Hardwoods used for tubs include oak, teak, and jarrah (the last is a little known Australian hardwood). Philippine mahogany (lauan) was also tried in the late 1970s, but without success. These tub woods have been chosen because they're resistant to decay and chemical damage; their strength and smooth, splinter-free surfaces also recommend them.

Redwood is probably the most widely used wood for hot tubs, especially along its native West Coast. It's extremely resistant to decay, does not splinter, and swells easily to watertightness. It is not extremely resistant to damage from caustic chemicals, however.

For strong, flawless staves and years of tubbing pleasure, make sure that the tub is built of clear, kiln-dried, vertical-grain heartwood (not the whitish sapwood). To accept less is to risk problems in the future. A well-maintained redwood tub will last about 15 years.

Cedar, the second most common tub wood, is similar to redwood in that both are porous softwoods. But cedar is slightly less resistant to decay and slightly more resistant to chemical damage. It also has a slightly shorter lifetime than redwood.

Oak, a strong durable hardwood, has a tendency to decay unless well maintained. It's widely available in the eastern United States and Canada, and is still used for wood barrels and casks.

Teak, the most expensive and elegant of hot tub woods, also lasts the longest—30 years or more. Its natural oiliness and density make it exceptionally resistant to water and chemical damage (which explains why it's used so much in boat building). Golden brown with dark streaking, teak is a strong, stable hardwood.

Jarrah, another dense hardwood, also makes for a long-lasting hot tub. (In Australia it's used for wine casks and pier pilings.) It is dark red in color.

A Look at Coopering

Like the barrels or casks from which they evolved, hot tubs are formed of vertical pieces of wood called staves.

The sides of the staves are bevelled to ensure a tight fit with their neighbors. A deep notch near the stave bottom, called a croze, fits it to the flooring; the lower lip of the stave is called its chine.

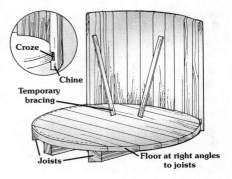

When all the staves are fitted at the croze and to each other, they're held together by from two to four steel hoops. The flooring rests on joists which, at the permanent site, in turn rest on a concrete slab.

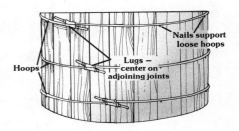

When the hoops are tightened by their lugs and the tub is filled with water, two forces make it watertight: the wood swells as it soaks up water, tightening the joints; at the same time, water pressure from within helps to align the staves.

Launching the Tub

In fact, the joints between the staves won't be perfectly watertight when the tub is first filled. You'll notice slight leaks until the wood has fully swollen, which may take about a week. If a leak becomes a gushing torrent, contact the manufacturer or your dealer; a torrent indicates improper milling or assembly.

Any slow, seeping leaks that don't disappear can usually be caulked with a good grade of plastic marine putty. Contact your dealer for other techniques, such as injecting epoxy into the croze.

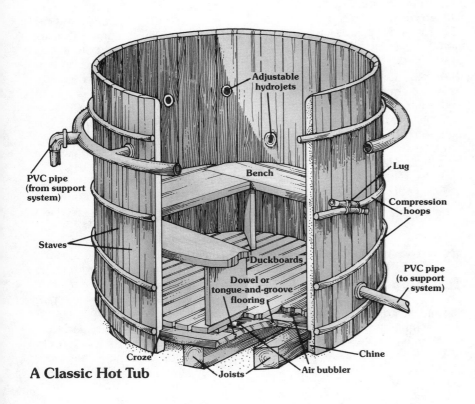

A Classic Hot Tub

Don't be alarmed when your new redwood tub leaches tea-colored tannin into the water. Though quite harmless to people, this heavy tannin may clog the tub's filter, so don't turn on any equipment yet. Instead, let the first tubful of water darken; then drain and wipe it out. Keep refilling and draining, running the filter for 2 to 3 hours per day, until the tannin has washed away. Soon the water will clear for a day or two, so you can enjoy a soak while the tannin continues to leach. After about a week, it should be gone. If you want to clear the water faster, use an oxidizer, available from most dealers.

Sizes and Seating

The deep, sheltered soak possible in a tub is one of the reasons why hot tub enthusiasts prefer the wood barrel. Although some spas use the full 24-inch maximum seat height (measured from the top of the seat to the lip), many do not, and their molded seats can't be adjusted like the wood supports of a hot tub's bench seats.

Typically, a small hot tub measures 3 or 4 feet high by 5 feet across and holds 325 to 500 gallons of water. A more generous tub with a height of 4 feet and a diameter of 6 feet holds 700 gallons. Five-foot-high tubs are also available.

A bench around the inside of higher tubs can hold from two to six people, depending on the tub's size (in shorter tubs, you sit on the floor). Benches should be attached to the tub with screws so they can be removed for maintenance and repair.

Hot Tub Pros and Cons

The popularity of the hot tub in the 1970s encouraged many entrepreneurs with little or no experience in manufacturing hot tubs to start up businesses to meet the demand. When interest in hot tubs slackened, many simply went out of business as fast as they had entered it. Consequently, when owners experienced problems with their tubs, they had no one to turn to.

And, inevitably, there were problems. Many of the early hot tubbers

apparently were not informed or did not understand the necessity of diligent maintenance. Even some owners who did keep up with good maintenance still found that their tubs started to leak after a few years of use. Often, the support equipment failed, due to improper use of chemicals, undersized components, or poor quality.

In any case, the reputation of hot tubs has suffered over the years. Some warn that tubs aren't sufficiently hygienic because the porous, organic wood used to make them provides lots of potential hiding places for bacteria. Others claim that chlorine and bromine, along with other chemicals used in maintenance, are likely to damage the wood when overused; still others complain that, sooner or later, tubs leak, inevitably and irreparably.

Proper maintenance and water chemistry can easily overcome the concerns about hygiene and chemical damage. Whether the vessel is a nonporous plastic spa or a soft, organic redwood cask, good maintenance is the only guarantee of clean, safe water. Also, if the proper maintenance program is followed faithfully, there should be no excess of chlorine in the water to damage the tub's wood. None of the woods used in hot tub construction is susceptible to chemical damage as long as a normal balance of chemicals is maintained.

As for leaks, once the tub's staves have had time to swell and make tight joints, a tub should not leak again if it has been built from the right kind of wood and properly assembled, installed, and maintained. If a tub does leak before the end of its expected lifetime, a good tub dealer can help out with a reliable product.

The Support System

Despite their different designs, both the spa (in-ground and portable) and the hot tub offer the same attraction—the hot, bubbly water that swirls inside each one.

What makes the hot water magic possible is the support system. A simple cluster of equipment, it circulates, heats, and filters the water, as well as sends it surging through hydrojets at great force. A functioning support system in a typical portable spa, called a skid pack, is illustrated on the opposite page. The system for a hot tub or in-ground spa is similar, only larger, and is housed a short distance away.

When you purchase a portable spa, the equipment is built in, so you have little, if any, choice. Part of your decision of which portable to buy should be based on the support equipment under its skirt. The quality of this equipment can vary a lot. For a hot tub or small in-ground spa, support equipment sometimes also comes in a preassembled skid pack like the one shown.

Larger support equipment, purchased separately, usually goes with a larger spa or hot tub installation. Your spa or tub dealer can make recommendations—leave sizing of equipment to these experts. But beyond this, the more you know about your choices and how each piece of equipment works, the more trouble-free pleasure you can expect from the spa or tub later on.

Obviously, a well-established, reliable manufacturer is one good indication of quality equipment. Since much of this hardware is just a scaled-down version of pool equipment, many manufacturers already have proven reputations.

Another indication of quality is the length and terms of guarantees; be suspicious of any short-term warranties. A UL listing (a listing with or recognition by the private Underwriters Laboratories) is a vitally important indication of safety; equipment that receives such a listing has to pass high standards of testing.

Also, check for quality materials—stainless steel and heavy-gauge plastics. Learn the names of top-quality manufacturers and look for their products in skid packs and in separate equipment packages.

Finally, compare basic specifications for similar products—for example, the kilowatt ratings of electric heaters, the BTU (British Thermal

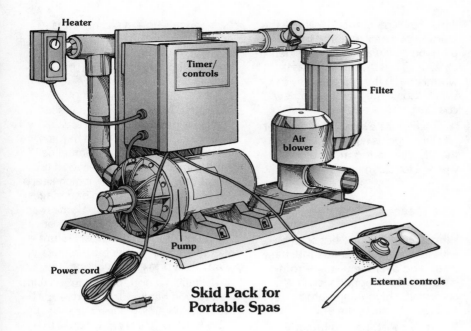

Skid Pack for Portable Spas

Labels: Heater, Timer/controls, Filter, Air blower, Pump, Power cord, External controls

Units) ratings of gas heaters, the square footage of filters, and the horsepower ratings of pumps. Though these numbers won't give you a precise evaluation of the efficiency or quality of each piece of equipment, they can provide you with a general basis for comparing one support system with another.

The Pump

The pump performs a critical function in keeping the water in a spa or hot tub moving.

Pumps move water by sucking it in one side and pushing it out the other. In a spa or tub, the pump propels the water with great force through hydrojets into the vessel. Then, it sucks water out through one or two drains

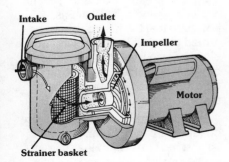

Labels: Intake, Outlet, Impeller, Motor, Strainer basket

Pump

and pumps it through the filter, then through the heater. Enroute, any leaves or debris become trapped in the pump's strainer basket.

Filtered and reheated to a preset temperature, the water is sent back again into the spa or tub through the hydrojets.

Though simple to describe, this is actually quite a complex job. For example, it takes much more power and speed for the pump to operate the hydrojets than it does to simply circulate water through the support system.

In addition, the pump's rate must match the filter's capacity to trap oils and organic particles efficiently. If the pump pushes water too fast or too slowly through the filter, the spa or tub won't be adequately cleaned.

The horsepower of the pump used on a particular spa or hot tub should correspond to its water volume and number of hydrojets. Typically, a 1 hp pump can handle a 500- to 700-gallon spa or tub that has four hydrojets.

Two-speed pumps have gained popularity as an energy-saving measure. For example, many portable spas use a ¾ hp pump that runs at two speeds. The higher speed is required to activate the hydrojets, which operate only while the spa is in use. The lower speed handles water

circulation through the heater and filter; it operates at significantly lower cost, keeping the water at the desired temperature, as well as sparkling clear and clean.

Larger in-ground spas often need a 1½ to 2 hp pump to handle the larger amount of water and to operate additional jets.

For spas with more than four jets, a two-pump system provides the best service. The smaller pump handles the relatively slow circulation through the filter and heater; the larger pump provides the main power to the hydrojets.

The Filter and Skimmer

Essential to good hygiene as well as to the upkeep and longevity of equipment, the filter removes dirt, algae, and other residue from spa or tub water. For a spa or tub whose support equipment is well matched to its size and that gets average use and regular chemical maintenance, a filtering cycle that operates at least 2 hours each day will keep the water clean.

Your dealer will probably advise you to run the filter more often at first, then gradually decrease the time periods as long as the water remains sparkling clean. Also, you should increase filtration time after heavy use of the spa or tub.

Typically, tubs are not equipped with skimmers, but these are becoming standard on spas. Acting as a surface filter, the skimmer catches leaves and other floating debris in its removable basket. This collector is particularly important if your spa remains uncovered for long periods of time or is located near trees that shed leaves, needles, or other debris.

Many skimmers on portable spas are combined with top-loading filters—a real convenience when the time comes to pull the filter for cleaning. Otherwise, you may have to drain the spa in order to clean the filter.

Several types of filters have been used for spas and hot tubs. Currently favored for its ease of maintenance is the cartridge type, which is available in a range of sizes.

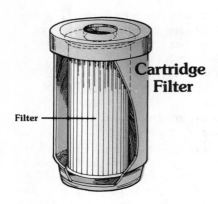

Cartridge Filter

Filter

Cartridge filters can handle approximately a gallon of water a minute per square foot of surface area. Made of nonwoven polyester, Dacron, or treated paper, their huge surface (typically between 25 and 50 square feet) is neatly drawn up in accordian pleats, forming the cylindrical cartridge (see illustration above). As water passes through, it leaves dirt, hair, oil, and other organic materials behind in the filter material.

The greater the square footage of the filter, the greater the volume of water it can handle per minute. Since the pump determines the rate of water flow, pump and filter sizes have to be carefully matched for the system to work properly. Choose the largest filter your equipment can handle.

Most cartridge filters lift out and clean easily with a garden hose or with cleaning fluid recommended by the manufacturer. If the spa or tub is used fairly often, check the filter once a week; you can tell by looking at it if it needs cleaning (about every 4 to 6 weeks.) Note that cartridge filters in some skid packs can only be checked and cleaned at the time you drain and clean your portable.

In a well-maintained system, a cartridge filter should last for a year or two before it needs replacement.

A *DE (diatomaceous earth) filter* is sometimes used with very large spas and hot tubs. It can handle a heavier load of dirt than a cartridge filter. The fine, chalky diatomaceous earth traps solids, providing the maximum filtration possible in the smallest surface.

Cleaning a DE filter is a more demanding process than cleaning a cartridge filter. Usually, the DE filter is backwashed by reversing the water

flow of the spa or tub. (Because the amount of water required to accomplish the backwashing is considerable, in all but the largest spas it would empty the spa completely.) When thoroughly washed, a new coating of DE is applied.

The *high-rate sand filter,* another efficient type, is used similarly to the DE filter. It, too, must be backwashed for cleaning.

The Heater

Where would a good hot soak be without a suitable heater? Much has been tried over the years—from solar energy to chopped wood—to achieve the high temperatures necessary for tubs and spas.

Today, most spa and tub buyers choose either a gas or an electric heater. No matter what your choice is, rely on your dealer to determine the correct size heater for your spa or tub, based on the number of people who will use the spa regularly, and how often and how long they'll be soaking. Be sure also that your electric heater is listed by Underwriters Laboratories (UL); gas heaters should be American Gas Association (AGA) approved.

Gas heaters. Where available, natural gas is traditionally the least expensive fuel. Propane is also an option in areas where natural gas isn't available.

Since gas heaters are typically much larger than their electric counterparts, for the quickest recovery—the briefest wait while the spa or tub

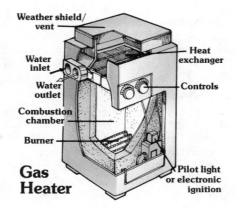

Weather shield/vent

Water inlet

Water outlet

Combustion chamber

Burner

Heat exchanger

Controls

Pilot light or electronic ignition

Gas Heater

water heats up—a gas heater is superior to even a 220-volt electric heater. You'll have to vent a gas heater, though, as well as run a gas line to it.

Electric heaters. For small spas (such as portables) and in areas where the kilowatt is still a bargain, electric heaters offer convenience and compact size. Unlike wood tubs, most spas are insulated, which keeps the cost of heating down and makes electricity more practical. Some manufacturers offer either 110-volt or 220-volt models, but most feature "convertibles"—electric heaters that can convert to either voltage.

Installing a portable equipped with a 110-volt heater typically does not require a building permit or inspection, since it is equipped with a cord (called a pigtail) with a standard plug for 110-volt house current. This plug-in feature is a big advantage, since the spa can be moved to a new location without the need for electrical work.

All you do is plug the spa in, after checking that the circuit is rated for 20 amps and that it's not already occupied by other heavy-draw applications. In areas that require a permit for a 110-volt spa, a dedicated circuit may be necessary. The circuit or outlet you're using will also have to be GFCI-protected if your spa isn't equipped with one of these devices.

Electric heaters of this type are very small—no more than a sealed, stainless-steel chamber the size of a large matchbox that contains a short resistance coil. As a result, their ability to heat water quickly is poor—less than 2 degrees per hour increase.

Nearly all 110-volt electric heaters are rated at 1.5kw, the greatest wattage that a 20-amp household circuit can safely handle. This means, however, that the heater cannot be turned on when the hydrojets and air blower are in use. This can be a serious drawback if the spa is being used for a long period of time or several times in an evening.

Well-insulated portables (for more on this, see page 21) can guard against heat loss when the spa is not in use, but long soaks and use of a blower produce a fairly rapid heat loss which can't be controlled by insulation.

Slow recovery is not a problem with 220-volt heaters. They're typically rated at 6kw, the increased voltage allowing for faster heating; also, the hydrojets and blower can be operated at the same time as the heater. However, 220-volt heaters have to be hard-wired—that is, permanently connected to a 220-volt circuit with a junction box. This requires an electrical permit and professional help, but it's a relatively simple procedure.

Electric heaters are also used as a backup to solar heating. Although heating swimming pools with the sun's energy has proven cost effective in some climates, the higher temperatures required by spas and hot tubs make it a far less effective heating method in these cases. At present, solar heating of tubs and spas serves primarily to reduce the cost of using electricity or gas. If you want to explore the solar heating option, consult a local solar company.

Other lesser-used fuels burned to heat spas and hot tubs include oil, wood, and coal. Another interesting approach is to install a heat exchanger. It takes advantage of the household hot water heater, diverting some of the heat of the water stored within it to the spa or tub water.

The exchange is accomplished by coils of tubing or a pipe outfitted with fins that transfers the heat of domestic water to spa water without mixing the two. Calculate operating costs carefully, since installation is usually quite expensive, and check to be sure these systems are allowed by local code.

Hydrojets

Powered by the pump, hydrojets provide the true massage action of a spa or hot tub. In the hydrojet, a high-pressured stream of water is mixed with air, then propelled into the spa or tub water, causing it to swirl and bubble. Each hydrojet transmits a torrent of 12 to 15 gallons of water a minute.

The number of jets and sophistication of design vary from one

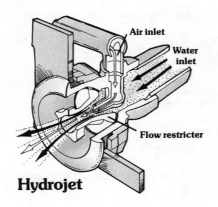

Hydrojet

(labels: Air inlet, Water inlet, Flow restricter)

manufacturer to another. If you're buying a hot tub, you can place jets almost anywhere. Given this flexibility, it makes sense to sit in the tub before it's fitted with jets so you can have them placed according to your height and preferences. Plastic spas offer less choice, but the better ones do allow you to find a spot within a larger reinforced panel.

One of the top-ranking spas can even be equipped with a hydrojet that moves up and down, creating a rippling massage, rather than focusing on just one area of the body.

Air intake in a hydrojet can be regulated by opening or closing the ports near the rim of the spa or tub. The best hydrojets are replaceable, adjustable for angle, and can be closed off completely (the spa may be fitted with four, but you may prefer to use only one, for example).

Just as some people like a gentler massage, others want a stronger one. Several manufacturers offer the option of diverting four regular hydrojets into one super, side-directed jet that spews out water at a rate of 90 gallons a minute. This transforms the spa into a version of the whirlpool bath—a form of therapy well known to athletes.

Air Blowers

Some spas and hot tubs are equipped with a small electric motor with a fan—called an air blower—that provides a gushing, tingling flow of bubbles up through the water. Air is sucked in from outside the spa or tub, then forcefully expelled through holes in the bottom of the vessel.

With proper sizing and installation, an air blower should give years of bubbling with no problems; little maintenance is required.

One serious drawback of blowers is that most use ambient air for the bubbles they spew out. If air temperature is cool, a blower can put a strain on your heater—or quickly turn the water tepid.

Another disadvantage to blowers is that they are usually quite noisy. Unlike a pump that works at around 3,400 RPM, a blower impeller turns at about 18,000 RPM—a speed that produces a loud, irritating whine.

Better-engineered blowers are quieter, but they can still be a mood-breaker when housed in hollow portables. With in-ground installations, you can place the blower and other support equipment at a far enough distance from the spa or tub to prevent noise distraction. Consider neighbors, too, when you're planning for a blower.

Controls

All spas and hot tubs are fitted with controls that allow you to operate the support equipment. Some controls only function manually; most spas and tubs, however, have some type of automatic controls as well.

Manual controls—to engage the pump (either for circulation or to power the hydrojets), to start up the blower, or to turn on the underwater light—are typically mounted on the rim of the spa or on the edge of the surrounding deck. These controls are either air switches (the action of depressing the button sends a column of air down a thin plastic tube to activate the switch) or touch-activated electronic switches.

Most spas and tubs are also equipped with some automatic controls. The simplest automatic device is a thermostatically controlled heater. Most 110-volt portables are controlled by a thermostat—water circulates through the filter and is heated whenever the temperature falls below the preset level. This typically keeps the water circulating for about 2 hours a day—sufficient for spas that are used a few times a week or less and remain covered between uses.

Gas-heated tubs and spas and 220-volt portables are usually equipped with a timeclock that controls filtration periods, since the time it takes to heat the water is so much less than in 110-volt units. With a timeclock, the heater cycles on and off in response to the thermostat during these filtration periods. By setting the timeclock to cycle on about 30 minutes or an hour before the time you typically use the spa each day, you can guarantee that a hot, clean tub will be waiting for you.

A new wrinkle that has become increasingly popular is a dual timeclock. The first clock has a 24-hour duration and is typically set to circulate the water at four different times during the day and night. (Try to schedule one to follow your last soak of the day).

The second clock has a 7-day duration and controls the heater. The longer time frame on the heater clock allows you to bring the tub up to temperature at one time during the week (after work for example) and at another time on weekends, when you're on a different schedule.

Most 110-volt portables aren't equipped with timeclocks because of their slow recovery time. But when you're away on vacation, it's possible to connect a timeclock to the plug-in cord of a portable, which will assure that the water is circulated several times a day even though the thermostat is turned down.

Controls are becoming more and more sophisticated in keeping with today's electronics revolution. For example, if you have an outdoor spa or tub, you can now install a convenient second control panel inside the house so you don't even have to go outside to fire things up. These remote panels often include digital readouts of water temperature and functions in operation. Some spas are even wired to accept the transmission of a remote controller similar to a garage door opener.

No matter how sophisticated the controls, all spas and tubs have a manual switch that can override your settings to turn the system on and off.

Beyond the Basic Equipment

The heater, pump, and filter represent the serious support system of a spa or hot tub. But a quantity of other equipment is also floating around in today's hot water marketplace. Some of these items are useful; others have been created purely for fun.

Protective Covers

So essential is a good cover to the overall safety and economy of a spa or tub that it really should be considered basic equipment.

Covering the spa or tub whenever it's not in use is extremely important. A cover's obvious function is protection. It keeps out curious children and pets, and prevents leaves and other debris from getting into the water and clogging the system. At the same time, a cover helps conserve the water's heat, which would otherwise rise and escape. Not covering the spa or tub for even one night will show up in higher utility bills.

Rigid covers. The best covers today are rigid ones made of foam—typically expanded polystyrene—covered with vinyl. Their insulation value ranges from R-10 to R-14. Many are hinged at the center for easier removal; others are formed of two and three pieces and connected by elastic straps.

Foam covers are lightweight, generally weighing 25 to 30 pounds. However, over time (a good cover will last for 5 or 6 years), the foam absorbs moisture, so eventually it will weigh a lot more.

To avoid trouble early on, buy the best cover you can. A good one will cost between 5 and 10 percent of the value of a typical portable spa, but it's a worthwhile investment.

There are many ways to judge quality in a cover. First, look at the thickness of the vinyl and the quality of its backing (avoid cotton backing—it won't stand up to the chemicals evaporating from the water). Second, check the stitching at seams and handles. Look for double or triple stitching and heavy-duty nylon zippers.

The thickness of the foam is also important. A 2-inch thickness is adequate for interior spas or tubs, but 3 inches is minimal for outdoor use. Make sure that the foam is tapered (for example, 3½ inches thick at the center of the cover, 2½ inches on the sides) so that rainwater can drain off the cover before its weight breaks the foam core.

Look for metal C-channels along the hinge—they give the foam extra rigidity. Also, if the foam is sealed in some way before it's clad with the vinyl, it will resist absorbing moisture for a longer period. Either way, there should be a grommeted drain hole on the underside of each section.

Most rigid covers come with tie-downs or other devices for battening them down securely against wind or curious children. You can also find

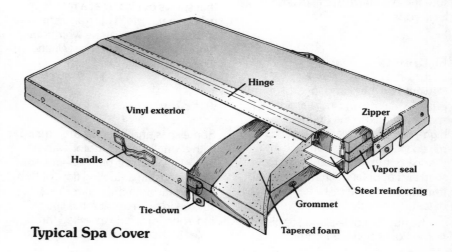

Typical Spa Cover

lockable covers and even some that have built-in alarms that sound if they are disturbed.

To make your rigid cover last longer, keep it waxed so that it will shed rain more easily. Also, wait at least 30 minutes after adding chemicals to the water before replacing the cover. And for safety's sake, *always* remove the entire cover before taking a soak.

Flexible covers. Lightweight alternatives to rigid vinyl covers are available if security and energy savings aren't very important to you. One, a simple bubble-plastic pad, floats on the water and can be used solo or in concert with a rigid cover for extra insulation.

Another type forms a big plastic bubble, or tent, over the water. This cover is designed to get a boost from the sun in keeping the water warm; it's not very effective in cold or cloudy weather.

Labor-Saving Sanitizers

Chlorinating a spa or tub doesn't demand a lot of time (see page 30), but it does require strict discipline—it's not a task you can put off until "next week." If you find this regimen too burdensome, you can use an automatic sanitizer.

The least expensive of these is a floating plastic dispenser filled with a stick sanitizer that leaches slowly into the water through a grid of holes (the size and number are adjustable). As you might imagine, this system is based on a very rough average of your tub or spa's needs and requires monitoring with a test kit.

Much more reliable (but also much more expensive) is an automatic feeder. This machine measures the free chlorine in the water and then emits as much additional chlorine as needed. It can do the same job with bromine. Apart from occasionally checking the water with a test kit and making sure that the bottle of sanitizer supplying the feeder hasn't been emptied, you can scratch chlorinating off your list.

Two other sanitizing techniques offer a partial alternative to chlorine or bromine: use of either ultraviolet light or ozone. Both of these systems should be backed up with small amounts of sanitizing chemicals to be safe and effective. Though both methods have an enthusiastic following, both have at least an equal number of detractors. Consult your dealer and then talk to people who have used such a system before you make up you mind.

Ultraviolet light has long been used by medical facilities as a germicide. The use of the light with a spa or tub is based on the same principle. Water is exposed to an ultraviolet light source (actually a long light bulb that lasts from 3 to 5 years) at a relatively slow rate of flow. Typically, a low-concentrate solution of hydrogen peroxide is used in the water as a sanitizer.

This system requires expert advice before installation, since the water chemistry is different from typical chlorine or bromine systems. It's important to be able to count on a full-service spa dealer to provide service and support once the system is running.

Ozone is another sanitizing agent. An ozone molecule is made up of three oxygen atoms. When mixed into spa or tub water, ozone oxidizes contaminants in much the same way chlorine- or bromine-based compounds do (they are oxidizers too, after all).

Ozone has been used for many years in Europe to sanitize large quantities of water, from public pools to drinking water. It leaves the water crystal clear with little chemical odor or irritation. But it's very expensive. As a relative newcomer in a marketplace dominated by pool and spa chemical companies, ozone hasn't yet gained widespread popularity. Also, an ozonator must be backed up with small amounts of chlorine or bromine.

Ozone can be created either by exposing air to ultraviolet light under controlled conditions (the UV method) or by passing electricity between metal plates (the corona discharge method). The latter method produces a good deal more ozone but is quite expensive. Again, setting up the equipment for either method requires professional advice and upkeep.

Environments to Go

Many spa and tub dealers sell wood components that you can wrap around your new purchase to create an instant outdoor environment.

Decking is almost as indispensible to spas and tubs as big, fluffy towels. Typically, large decks are built from scratch on site, but some portable spa dealers offer deck segments that will fit around your spa. This is particularly useful if your portable is oddly shaped or is slightly curved in profile. You can also purchase benches and steps from some dealers.

In some situations, shelter overhead provides as much needed comfort as smooth decking underfoot. Like the lacy gazebo of Victorian times, lath shelters of redwood and cedar have become popular accessories for spas and hot tubs. Providing just enough privacy, the gazebo also admits light, air, and refreshing glimpses of the outside world.

All these environmental extras come either in kit form or assembled. Be sure that the wood is all cedar or redwood heartwood, unless you plan to paint.

Other landscaping ideas for spas and tubs appear on pages 22–28.

Night Lighting

Many hot water enthusiasts prefer to indulge after nightfall or while it's raining or snowing. Also, because spas and tubs are so much fun for guests, much soaking goes on during the evening. At these times, adequate lighting is an important safety consideration.

Today, many spas come with built-in, low-voltage lights. But be sure also to light steps, deck edges, and other potentially hazardous places. Outdoor lamps that are low to the ground are sufficient—and allow more privacy. But for a little outdoor drama, consider backlighting a nearby tree or shrub as well.

Simple, low-voltage outdoor lighting kits work well around spas and tubs. They come with cable and a transformer. Whatever lights you use, be sure they have an Underwriters Laboratories (UL) listing.

Accessories for Work and Play

Though they're not necessary, cleaning gadgets sold for pools, such as special vacuum cleaners and scrubbing brushes, can also be used in a spa or tub.

Inflatable vinyl pillows can add comfort to your soak. If you like to stretch out completely, there's even a spa lounge made of vinyl.

A number of practical items are available in buoyant form. A floating digital thermometer can provide an instant readout of water temperature. Floating plastic trays keep food and drink (noncrumbly snacks, such as apple and cheese chunks, and non-alcoholic beverages) comfortably within reach. And, inevitably, you can even buy a hot-water floating cassette player that's stereophonic and water resistant.

For more water play, consider tinting or scenting the spa or tub water with special additives. Using a packaged kit, you can also transform your spa or tub into a fountain. For additional ideas, visit your local spa or tub dealer.

Before You Buy

From chlorine to kilowatts to electronic controls, today's spa and hot tub confront the consumer with more technical detail than might be evident at first glance.

Because the spa and hot tub industry is still young, it's awash with changes and improvements. Although the reliability of many of its products has been proven through years of service in the swimming pool industry, the quality of its newest technology is, of course, untested. This is why it can literally pay you, or save you disappointment, to learn as much as possible before purchasing.

Be as cautious about buying a spa or tub and its support equipment as you would be about buying a new car. Find out as much as you can in advance; make thoughtful, rather than impulsive, decisions. Though you can always sell a car later, it's a lot harder to unload a used tub.

Assessing Your Needs

Before you start shopping, think about your situation and your preferences. Do you want to soak in a hot tub—or in a spa? (The major differences are outlined on page 6. Also, note the more detailed descriptions of spas and hot tubs in this chapter and the color photographs that start on page 33.) Sound out friends who own one or the other. You may want to visit a dealer's showroom just to look around.

Think, too, about the number of people who will be soaking at one time. Do you plan to use the spa or tub socially, or will it be a more private experience? The answer to this question will guide you to the right choice of shell size, seating arrangement, and heater.

If you expect to do a lot of entertaining, you'll probably also want to envision decking, lighting, and landscaping around the spa or tub.

Which is best for you, an indoor or outdoor site? Obviously, climate and privacy considerations may lead you to choose an indoor spa or tub; if so, you'll come up against the difficulty of dealing with high humidity and the weight of a spa or tub filled with water.

For an outdoor spa or tub, consider how close you want it to your house and where you will place the support equipment. Also, be sure to take into account sun and wind patterns, as explained on page 25.

Finding a Reliable Dealer

To locate dealers, ask friends for recommendations or look in the Yellow Pages of your telephone directory under "Hot Tubs" or "Spas."

Here are a few guidelines for choosing a reliable dealer. They can't

absolutely guarantee your satisfaction, but they do indicate high business standards.

• Spas and tubs should be the dealer's main business, not just a sideline. A full-time dealer is most likely to be knowledgeable, as well as reliable in the future if you ever need service.

• Find out how long the dealer has been in the spa or tub business under the same name, at the same location.

• Be sure that the dealer's products—spa shells, tubs, support equipment, and other accessories come from established manufacturers with proven reputations.

• Check with the Better Business Bureau in your area to find out if any complaints have been registered against the dealer.

• Ask the dealer for at least two references of previous clients, so you can see their installations and hear about their experience.

• Find out if the dealer belongs to the National Spa and Pool Institute, which sets industry standards.

Some dealers just sell spas and tubs and their support equipment. A full-service dealer, on the other hand, not only sells you what you need but also is licensed to install the equipment, and design and install the surrounding landscape. A dealer can also obtain all necessary permits.

Finding Reliable Products

The only way you can be assured of choosing quality products is to find out all you can about them first. Simply by asking thoughtful questions and listening carefully to the answers, you can often tell whether or not a dealer feels confident about a product's reliability. This is also a good opportunity to ask the dealer about the services he offers as a retailer, as well as specific questions on delivery, installation, and warranties. Here are ten questions that will get you started.

1. What kind of warranty comes with the spa shell or hot tub and the support equipment? Ask the dealer how a warranty claim is made and whether the dealer will back up the manufacturer's promises with a writ-

ten warranty of the dealer's own. (This way, if either the dealer or the manufacturer goes out of business or otherwise fails you, you're still covered by the other.)

For more information about warranties, see the box at right.

2. Does the spa carry the seal of the International Association of Mechanical Plumbing Officials (IAMPO)? Does support equipment (both remote and portable) carry the Underwriters Laboratories (UL) listing? Both IAMPO and UL subject equipment to tough testing.

3. Does the dealer charge for delivery? Get a written agreement on exactly how and where the spa or tub will be delivered, down to such details as removing gates, fences, etc.

4. Will the dealer provide written directions and all chemicals needed for good maintenance? Will the dealer answer your questions in the future, or make a house call after your spa or tub goes home? Be sure to ask the dealer to review every step of good maintenance with you.

5. If the spa is acrylic, how thick is the sheet used in its manufacture? If it is only ⅛ inch thick, it is too thin and may not hold up over time; however, very thick acrylic isn't good either. Its rigidity eliminates the slight flex that is necessary in a spa shell. Inspect an acrylic spa carefully for fractures, chips, or delaminated spots before you buy it.

6. If you're buying a portable spa, how thick is the wood that makes up the skirt? It can vary from a scant ⅜ inch to a fairly sturdy ¾ inch. Look for good quality wood and craftsmanship. The door should be mounted on a sturdy hinge and provide access to all the components. A wood base that's recessed and treated will prevent rotting and insect damage.

7. For a portable, how thick is the foam insulation sprayed inside? Some cabinets are completely filled, providing excellent insulation for both the spa and supply pipes, as well as greater structural stability. This degree of insulation results in lower energy costs, but plumbing connections must be tested first, since these will be inaccessible once the foam is applied.

Warranty Protection

The hot water industry today is changing rapidly. As a result, the consumer is benefitting from new, improved products and designs. But a degree of caution and a measure of protection are also needed in the cases where designs and materials haven't yet met the test of time.

Choosing a reputable dealer who is up-to-date on changes in the industry is a good precaution. Your real protection, however, comes from the warranties supplied by manufacturers. Ask to see these warranties before you commit to buying the product. Read them carefully and ask your dealer to answer any questions that arise.

You should also discuss your responsibility in keeping the warranty in force. No spa or hot tub can be expected to perform trouble-free if it's abused or if proper maintenance is neglected. Most spa manufacturers warranty different parts of their spas for different periods of time. They break down like this:

Spa surfaces. Because of problems with acrylic finishes, most manufacturers have reduced the number of years on their warranties from as many as 10 to as few as a year or two. Consider a year as a minimum and look for more.

Some of the high-impact plastic spa shells, such as ROVEL®, are warrantied for up to 5 years.

Remember, however, that a warranty is only good if the manufacturer is still in business to honor it. As a rule of thumb, the manufacturer offering the warranty should have been in business at least as long as the warranty period promised. It's also a good idea to speak with your dealer about the financial stability of the manufacturer and how quickly and effectively the manufacturer responds to claims.

One of the important points to look at with any warranty is whether the claims will be satisfied in the field or whether the product has to be shipped back to the manufacturer (typically at the owner's expense). Another is the question of who performs the warranty service—the dealer or a factory representative. Patching acrylic is tricky and not all dealers have this capability. You may want to ask your dealer how quickly a manufacturer's representative will respond.

It's also worth discussing with your dealer whether the manufacturer you're considering will replace the spa shell upon a serious complaint or will simply repair it. Obviously, no manufacturer will replace your spa if a small blister shows up after a while. A large blister, however, will encourage delamination, which would require replacement of the spa.

Structural elements. With acrylic or the newer plastic shells, structural integrity is seldom a problem. Most manufacturers offer warranties of at least 5 years. This warranty does not cover problems with in-ground spas that shift or settle; that's part of the contract warranty you have with the person who installed your spa.

Equipment. Look for a minimum one-year warranty on equipment (pumps, filters, heaters, blowers, and controls). Be sure that this period covers both parts *and* labor (some manufacturers only offer 90 days on labor). Also confirm before you buy that you won't have to disconnect and send in defective equipment to get warranty service.

To find out about comparative operating costs for various models, ask to see documentation so you can make comparisons.

8. What kind of heater is offered? On a portable, does it have a convertible electric heater that will allow you to change from 110 to 220 volts in the future? How fast will the heater raise the water temperature by 20 degrees?

9. If the filter is the cartridge type, how big is it? One that's 25 square feet is very skimpy, which means more frequent cleaning; 50 square feet is better. Is the filter easy to remove? Do the controls give you the option of running the circulation/filtration only, so that you don't have to heat the water while you're on vacation?

10. Are the hydrojets adjustable and/or replaceable? Can you shut them down selectively? Are they positioned correctly for your body? (Only you can answer this, by trying them out.) How much noise do the hydrojets and blower make when operating together?

Locating and Landscaping Your Spa or Tub

However much pleasure a spa or tub brings while it is being used, it remains a dramatic feature of the landscape during all the other hours of the day. For this reason, it needs to look like more than an oversized wash basin or a puddle.

How to achieve a handsome setting raises a host of questions. For many homeowners, a basic necessity is comfortable sitting or sprawling space right next to the spa. Decks and patios become both a requirement and an opportunity to build attractive changes of level into the environment. They also allow this area to play host to other activities.

In some climates, what goes overhead is even more important to comfort than what lies underfoot. Sheltering devices can make even bolder statements than decks.

Dealing with Grade

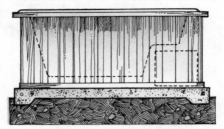
Spa on Level Ground

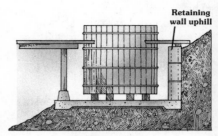
Hillside Tub

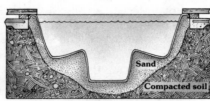
Spa in Level Ground

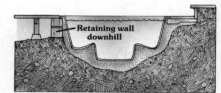
Hillside Spa

Still more important than any visual detail is the need to locate the spa or tub where it can be used most comfortably.

One of the usual distinctions between going for a swim and taking a hot soak is that you are less likely to wear a suit for the latter. If this is a factor, the spa or tub might fit your plans better if it is close to the house—or even indoors—rather than clear at the back corner of the property. You will also have to consider the height of neighboring houses.

In the following pages we try to address most major landscaping questions to help you assess your individual opportunities.

As a first step, check into local zoning requirements concerning setbacks, height limitations, and related legal limits. One other important legal consideration is that spas and tubs should have secure covers to keep children out of the water when they are not supervised. Courts have held that pools, spas, and similar bodies of water are attractive nuisances and that fencing alone is not a legally adequate barrier to a child. Some spa and tub covers have locks to meet this express situation, or you can outfit your spa or tub with a simple padlock system yourself.

Dealing with Grade

One of the complicating factors in picking a site for your spa or hot tub is the existing grade of your lot. Setting a portable spa, hot tub, or in-ground spa on or in level ground is relatively straightforward. But if the site is sloped—even a few inches for every horizontal foot—installation becomes a good deal more complicated and expensive.

As the two left-hand drawings above show, a portable spa or hot tub on level ground needs only a reinforced concrete slab. An in-ground spa requires digging a hole large enough to accommodate the shell and lining it with sand.

Hillside sites pose special construction problems, as the drawings on the right illustrate. For a portable spa or hot tub, a level cut has to be made in the hillside and a retaining wall built to hold it up. Any retaining wall over a few feet high should be engineered by a professional. A slab made of reinforced concrete is then poured to support the portable or hot tub.

An in-ground spa on a hillside also requires a retaining wall, but one on the downhill side. The wall supports the spa shell and helps to contain the sand base on which the shell rests.

A hillside installation also calls for the construction of an elevated deck around the spa or hot tub.

Where Will a Spa or Tub Work Best for You?

Budget yourself a block of time to find the right setting for your spa or tub. There are advantages to both indoor and outdoor locations—choose the one that suits your needs and budget, as well as your climate and landscape.

When picking an out-of-doors spot for your spa or tub (for indoor spas, see page 28), make a scale drawing of your property like the ones shown at right. On a sheet of graph paper show the following features:

• Lot dimensions.

• Location of house on lot (including doors and windows and the rooms from which they open).

• Points of the compass—north, south, east, and west.

• Path of the sun and any hot spots it produces.

• Utilities (water, gas, and sewers) and underground wires that could affect your spa or tub location. (Units never should be located beneath utility wires.)

• Setback boundaries (your city or county building department can tell you what they are).

• Direction of prevailing winds.

• Existing garden structures.

• Existing plants and trees.

• Problems beyond the lot line which may affect sun, view, or privacy, such as unsightly telephone wires, major plantings, or a neighbor's second-story window.

If you live on a sloping lot, it's also a good idea to draw a second map showing the lot's contours, high and low spots, and natural drainage.

With your "base map" drawn, cover it with tracing paper and try out your ideas. As you sketch, think about ease of installation, the visual effect in the garden or from indoors, and climate and terrain factors that will influence an outdoor site. Consider, too, the traffic patterns likely to be followed by bathers.

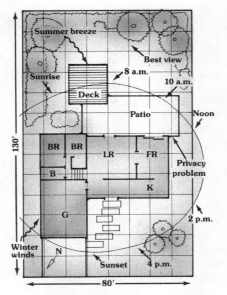

Getting a plan on paper is your first step in choosing an outdoor location for your spa or hot tub. Using graph paper, make a scale drawing of your property; show lot dimensions, house location, plants, trees, and garden structures, and any weather or privacy problems that might interfere with your hot bath enjoyment.

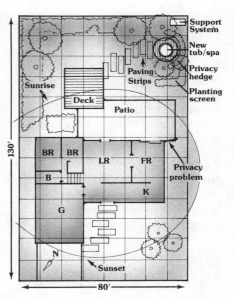

Sample plan, sketched on tracing paper placed over the scale drawing, shows one way a spa or tub might fit into an existing landscape. Located in a seldom-used corner of the lot, the spa becomes an eye-catching focal point. Screened with trees and a hedge, it is protected from wind, afternoon sun, and neighbors' lines of vision.

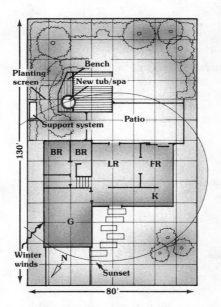

Alternate plan connects the new tub/spa to an existing low-level deck. Here, in an intermediate zone of the yard, the tub is near enough the house to be easily accessible, far enough away to remain a significant visual element in the garden. With a wood lid and benches, the spa unit doubles as an outdoor entertaining area.

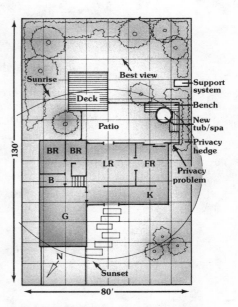

Tub/spa located nearest the house has the advantage of a sunny southern exposure, less costly installation (shorter plumbing and wiring distances), and easy access during wintry days when the tub or spa is most likely to be used. Closeness to household noise, however, can make it seem less like a private retreat and reduce tubbing's relaxing benefits.

Making the Most of an Odd-shaped Lot

One of the secrets of landscaping—whether you're incorporating a spa or tub into an existing garden or planning a garden from scratch—is knowing how to turn liabilities into assets. Awkwardly shaped lots, small garden spaces, and steeply sloping sites all depend on design imagination to make them work.

For the square-shaped lot shown at right, for instance, a circular approach relieves the strong angular lines of house and lot. To give the yard a longer look, focal points lie at each end: a hot tub is tucked into a circle of trees at one, a garden greenhouse at the other.

Primary drawbacks to the wedge-shaped lot below were its sharply angled corners and unequally divided outdoor spaces. The solution to the sharp corners was plantings to camouflage and soften them; the solution to the irregular outdoor spaces was to make one of them open and expansive, the other more private and sheltered—a perfect setting for spa or tub.

Study these approaches to making the best use of space in four typically odd-shaped lots: they illustrate how effective design can minimize eccentric features in a landscape. (Arrows on the drawings indicate the direction in which a viewer's attention is drawn by the various landscape elements.)

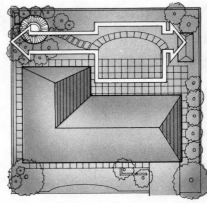

Square lot's rear garden *is made to seem less square with arc in lawn, and longer with focal points at each end. Leaving the house, one may look left toward the spa, which is sheltered in a circle of trees (and accessible from the main patio or master bedroom), or right toward a garden greenhouse.*

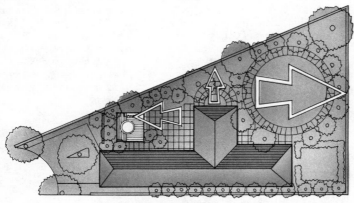

In a wedge-shaped lot, *irregular outdoor spaces lend themselves nicely to distinct activity zones. A generous open lawn area in one corner provides plenty of play space; a small patio area in another provides a more private climate for tubbing. Plantings soften the lot's sharp corners.*

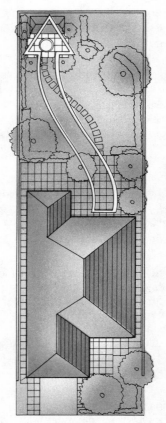

Long, narrow lot *has a barber-pole look to it unless its space can be divided into at least two distinct, offset areas. Here, an S-curved axis leads the eye across one garden to an open-air spa and spa-side shelter. A modest grade in this type of lot can add visual interest with different horizontal levels.*

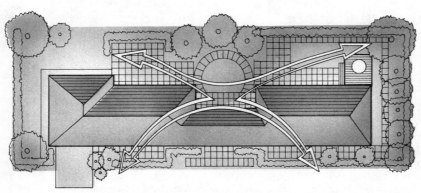

To give an extremely shallow lot *a feeling of greater depth, create focal points at the lot line with built-in benches, garden walks, or eye-catching plantings. Where setback limitations thwart you, break up the yard's length with a series of outdoor living areas. In the yard shown above there are four, with the spa at one end.*

Consider Your Climate

Evaluate climate conditions peculiar to your property before you install a spa or tub outdoors. Understanding seasonal sun and wind patterns that affect your lot will help you choose a setting that maximizes your hot bath enjoyment.

The seasonal sun. You've probably noticed that the sun generates varying amounts of shade on your property according to its seasonal position in the sky (*see illustrations below*). In the winter, shadows on the north side of the house are deeper, in the summer much shorter. Deciduous trees provide an exception, since they are bare in winter.

The Sun by Seasons

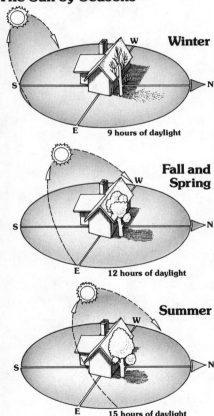

Winter

9 hours of daylight

Fall and Spring

12 hours of daylight

Summer

15 hours of daylight

Tracking sun daily and seasonally will help you determine whether a site is primarily sunny or shady. Expect long shadows (particularly in winter) from house, fences, and trees on north side of house. On south side, use a trellis to block out high, summer sun but allow low winter sun to penetrate.

As a general rule, a spa or tub situated on the north side of the house will almost always be in shade—an advantage if you live in a hot desert climate and want to protect your spa from the sun's hot midsummer rays.

If yours is a cool climate, the best setting for your spa or tub may be on the south side of the house, where it can take advantage of full sun. A spa or tub on the east side receives morning sun, and one on the west, sun in the afternoon.

Dealing with winter. Spas and tubs can be kept usable during winter at the expense of extra hours of heater use. When the weather does not lend itself to outdoor soaking, the heater thermostat should be lowered to a temperature too cool for a bath but warm enough to safeguard the spa or tub and its support system plumbing from freezing. During the coldest periods, adjust your controls for more frequent circulation.

During severe freezes, all support systems should be drained even if they're insulated and/or sheltered. Spas also should be drained, but tubs cannot be allowed to dry. (A tub should never be left without water for more than 2 days.) Tubs must be plumbed to allow draining the support system without draining the tub.

One other cautionary note: In snow country, do not place spas or tubs beneath eavelines: falling snow can crush them.

Dealing with wind. Next, study wind patterns around your house and lot. Too much wind blowing over your spa or tub on a cool day can be as unpleasant as no wind at all on a hot summer day. Excess wind around a spa also can kick up enough dust to tax its filter and pump, encourage evaporation, and cool the water temperature.

To pinpoint wind currents in your yard, try posting small flags where you want wind protection and observe their movements during windy periods. Observe, too, in the illustrations at right the effects different barriers have on wind to learn which type of fence or screen will protect you best while still meeting your aesthetic needs.

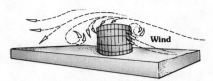

Unchecked exposure to wind rapidly cools the water in a spa or tub, kicks up dust, and puts an unnecessary strain on the support system.

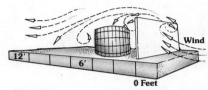

Wind washes over a solid fence as a stream of water would wash over a solid barrier. At about the distance equal to fence height, protection drops rapidly.

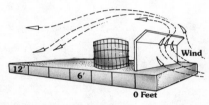

Angling a baffle into the wind gives greatest protection close to the fence, but effective protection also extends to a distance more than twice fence height.

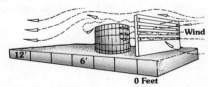

To break wind flow, choose a fence with laths spaced ½ inch apart, or screens of plants. Up close, the fence offers relatively little protection; temperatures are warmest at a distance equal to about twice fence height. Shrubbery, if dense, would yield more shelter.

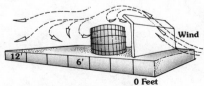

A 45° baffle at the top of a fence eliminates the downward crash of wind. You feel warmest in the pocket below the baffle and about 6 feet from the 6-foot-high fence. Beyond that point, temperature change is minimal.

How to Frame Your Spa or Tub

Except on rare occasions, your spa or hot tub needs a setting like a painting needs a frame. Of course, if your garden happens to be a grove of redwood trees, a spa standing among them will look perfect. But if you're planning to install a spa in a less dramatic setting, you need to think about an appropriate frame, wood or masonry, that will integrate it into the landscape in a pleasing way.

To decide whether you want your spa or tub to serve as a major focal point or as a more subtle element in the landscape, consider how it will affect the overall appearance of the yard. Will it complement or compete with other features—a handsome patio or deck, gazebo, or swimming pool? Will an above-grade spa overwhelm nearby low-growing plants you prize or will it balance garden plantings? Will it blend or clash with the architecture of your house?

If you choose to make your spa a garden focal point, consider placing it above grade and framing it with built-in benches. If you want a more subtle effect, install it flush with deck-ing or paving. If you install it above ground, it can still be made to seem unobtrusive if you soften it with plants.

The material you use to frame your spa or tub can make a big difference in its look and feel. Wood is easy to work and can be arranged in interesting patterns. Masonry, such as brick, pavers, natural stone, and nonskid tile, can also look very attractive and is splinter-free, but it can get very hot in open sunlight. Your choice, in part, will be based on what material best integrates the spa or tub with the site.

Raised decking, built-in benches, and existing evergreens provide a balanced setting for portable spa, situated in a seldom-used corner of the lot.

Rimmed with tile, this in-ground spa is surrounded by a simple, bold frame of sun-warmed flagstones.

Installed flush with a new deck, tub sits halfway above an existing brick patio. Design: Don Brandeau.

Concrete spa is separated from adjoining swimming pool by a broad tile seat. Design: Don Brandeau.

Hillside deck provides a handsome match of water and wood. Design: Chaffee-Zumwalt Assoc.

Gaining a Sense of Shelter

If your spa or tub is outdoors and you live in a temperate climate, there's usually no need to provide overhead protection. Periodic hot soaks in the rain are, for many people, wonderfully refreshing. But if you live in an area such as the Northwest, where rain is a dependable constant during long winter months—or if the sun beats a hot path to your spa in the summer—you may wish to cover it with a more substantial roof.

The illustrations below suggest a few of your many options. With the sky as their canopy, owners of the open-air situation have the advantage of stargazing at night and sky-gazing in the afternoon. Only a long stretch of hard rains keeps them from the pleasures of a good hot soak. Owners of the spa below prefer an open-air setting, although they added a dressing room to their sauna so rainy-day tubbers and sauna bathers would have a sheltered spot to cool down.

Between no roof and a solid roof lies a compromise—lath or lattice structures, such as the one at bottom right, that admit the sun but give a feeling of protection. You also can often buy prefabricated lath structures for spas and tubs from local dealers. One flexible solution is the removable umbrella, illustrated below left.

For solid protection you can go as far as a shingle-roofed gazebo that offers permanence as well as protection from sun and rain. Or you can shelter your spa with an airy greenhouse-style glass roof (below) that keeps out the rain but lets in the light—a decided disadvantage if you live in a climate where the sun makes the area uncomfortably hot.

Solid-roofed gazebo, *offering permanent shelter from sun and rain, becomes focal point of garden. Design: Lyman Seely.*

Adjoining sauna/dressing room *is handy when rainy-day bathers need a sheltered spot to cool down.*

Tempered glass *in a wood frame gives rain protection without shutting out the light or overhead view. Design: Brad Brown.*

Simple spa umbrella *shades your soak on a sunny day; when not needed, simply furl and store.*

Lath roof *provides partial shade and a sense of shelter for hillside spa. Design: Donald G. Boos.*

Screening for Weather and Privacy

Vertical screens—made from wood, canvas, glass, bamboo, plastic, or plants—can make a big contribution where you need privacy or wind protection. Depending on their design and location (and your climate—see page 25), vertical screens will modify wind, ensure privacy, block sun, muffle noise from neighbors, and—in the case of spas and tubs—separate them from more prominent areas of the garden.

With climate as your guide, determine which type of screen best suits your needs. A solid wood screen like the one shown below, for example, offers maximum privacy but minimum wind protection for the close-by tub.

If you need privacy for a spa in a shaded corner of the garden, consider using translucent white fiberglass in a wood frame. It can screen out a neighbor's line of sight without cutting out the light.

Where you wish to block wind without losing a view, consider using clear plastic or tempered glass panels.

Many of the most appealing screens are created with plants and trees. They give a soft, natural feeling to a spa or tub setting while they work to help disperse brisk winds, protect from hot sun, cushion noise, and cool the climate around them. You can screen with evergreen shrubs, vines on wood trellises—almost anything—although you should choose plants according to their growth rate, ultimate size, texture, color, shape, and habit. Avoid those that attract bees or shed debris over the area.

An Indoor Spa or Tub

Some spa and tub enthusiasts prefer an indoor setting, for several reasons.

There's the obvious advantage of having the spa or tub sheltered and accessible day and night, year-round. (In harsh climates, it's often necessary to have an indoor site that allows complete control over the environment—not only of the water, but also of the support system plumbing.)

Where privacy is essential but impossible to achieve in the garden, the house will provide it.

Where the safety of children—especially neighborhood children—is difficult to assure at an outdoor site, lockable doors solve all manner of legal and personal worries.

Compelling as one or more of these reasons may be, they do not make it any less difficult to locate a spa or tub inside. Integrating a spa or tub into household routine takes a good deal of thought. As one side effect, these vessels are marvelously efficient manufacturers of humidity—a plus if you live in a dry climate where air moisture is a scarcity, an uncomfortable handicap if your air is characteristically heavy with humidity.

Deciding on an indoor location. As anyone who has had to fit a new bed into a well-ordered house knows, an object 5 feet across cannot be slipped into a place unnoticed. When it is for such a singular purpose as a spa or tub is, the task of fitting it

Solid wood fence frames portable spa and provides privacy by screening out a neighbor's view.

Louvered fence modifies wind and blocks neighbor's line of sight without cutting off the view.

Lattice screen, designed to separate tub area from rest of garden, is softened with colorful vine. Design: Donald G. Boos.

Walls of wood-framed glass surround view-oriented tub to give tubbers and plants wind protection. Doors slide open and shut on tracks.

Shaping the Indoor Setting

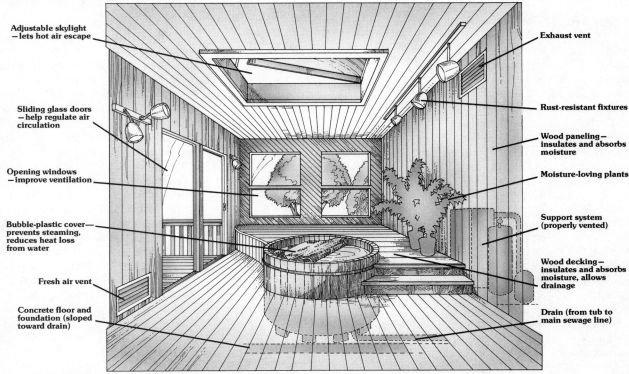

Adjustable skylight — lets hot air escape

Sliding glass doors — help regulate air circulation

Opening windows — improve ventilation

Bubble-plastic cover — prevents steaming, reduces heat loss from water

Fresh air vent

Concrete floor and foundation (sloped toward drain)

Exhaust vent

Rust-resistant fixtures

Wood paneling — insulates and absorbs moisture

Moisture-loving plants

Support system (properly vented)

Wood decking — insulates and absorbs moisture, allows drainage

Drain (from tub to main sewage line)

Consider all the above elements when you plan an indoor spa or tub. Under normal use, spas and tubs create enormous vapor clouds; if yours is indoors, you need to build a room around it that can manage a marine climate. In addition to wood, ceramic tile is often used as an indoor spa flooring material.

into a working household becomes doubly difficult.

Think first of traffic patterns. To be an oasis of calm, the spa will have to be away from the comings and goings of people in a hurry. This means putting it in a room that does not carry through traffic or serve several other purposes.

Try to locate your spa near a dressing area; trails of water across the house can be a nuisance to clean up. Consider locating it within reasonable reach of the outdoors. Even a nook-size deck or patio nearby can provide a pleasant place to relax.

Construction concerns. Once the problems of location are solved, the special requirements of construction must be faced. Weight and humidity are the two most complex and vital concerns.

Standard floors are designed and built to support 40 pounds per square foot. A small spa or hot tub filled with water and two adult bathers can easily apply 250 pounds to

the same square foot. For this reason, it's critically important to provide an adequate foundation. To support a spa safely, an existing wood frame floor (say in a spare bedroom) usually requires re-engineering; often, even a concrete slab in the basement must be replaced with a thicker, reinforced slab.

The requirements your building code sets for an indoor spa or tub's foundation, plumbing, and wiring—coupled with the need for efficient ventilation—explain why the best time to think about an indoor spa is prior to new home construction or room addition. Major remodeling within an existing building is unquestionably the most problematical route to a hot soak.

In addition to the need for an adequate substructure, flooring should slope toward a drain and be constructed of such materials as ceramic tile, sheet vinyl, concrete, flagstone, or masonry—materials that aren't affected by large doses of water. (Wood decking, constructed above a

concrete slab or drain field, also makes a satisfactory flooring for indoor spas. It absorbs some moisture, allows excess to drain through, and provides limited soundproofing.)

Walls and ceilings must have insulation with a vapor barrier to resist moisture. (This applies to interior as well as exterior walls.) The rest of the house also needs protection from the excess humidity produced by a spa.

Controlling condensation. Efficient ventilation is your best means of controlling the condensation that can collect on walls, windows, and ceiling, even when the spa is not in use.

To have maximum control over your indoor climate, it may be necessary to back up natural cross-ventilation with a forced air system.

In addition to ventilation, plan on double-glazed windows and skylights that inhibit condensation. Moisture-loving plants and walls paneled with unfinished wood are useful because they absorb excess moisture.

Maintenance: A Must

Bubbling over with good, clean fun, spas and hot tubs offer hours of relaxation and enjoyment. But in exchange, both demand a regular schedule of maintenance carried out conscientiously.

Obviously, the water must be kept clean. As part of your maintenance program, make it a rule that everyone shower with soap before entering your spa or tub. Be sure also to rinse thoroughly and not to use any lotions or suntan products—these can clog the filter. Never leave a bar of soap near the spa or tub.

Few people realize, at first, the load placed on the small water volume of a spa or tub by a simple, sociable soak. According to the National Spa and Pool Institute, five people bathing in a spa containing 500 gallons of water equals a crowd of 250 in an average-size, 25,000-gallon swimming pool.

To add to the load, the popular spa and tub water temperatures of 100° to 104°F/38° to 40°C encourage bacterial activity and risk of human infection.

These are the basic reasons why the water chemistry of a tub or spa can change very quickly—and, therefore, should be checked *every few days*, and *always* after heavy use.

Water Care Basics

Adequate maintenance of spa or tub water assures both good sanitation and proper water chemistry. Both are important to people's health and comfort, as well as to the longevity of the tub or spa and of its support equipment.

Sanitation is commonly achieved by adding chlorine or bromine to the water. Chlorine, sold in liquid, tablet, or granulated form, attacks and destroys bacteria and algae. This process, however, uses up a portion of the added chlorine. What remains after the battle of the bacteria is fought and won is known as *free chlorine*.

Each day, as you check the water, you measure how much free chlorine remains, which tells you how much more you need to add. Ideally, the tested water will show 3.0 to 5.0 parts per million of free chlorine. (Test kits for this procedure are explained on page 31.)

Bromine disinfects water as effectively as chlorine. You can buy it in sticks, tablets, or as a dry mixture that's applied in two steps.

Bromine evaporates less quickly than chlorine at high water temperatures and is more effective at higher pH levels. However, it has the same nasty habit of forming chemical compounds (called *bromamines*) when the pH is allowed to drop too low. These are very irritating to the skin and eyes. For more on this and the chlorine equivalent (*chloramines*), see the boxed feature on the facing page.

In addition to your regular maintenance, many chemical companies, along with tub and spa dealers, recommend that you superchlorinate, or *shock*, the water once *every week*. This kills stubborn algae that have learned to resist the normal, relatively scanty amount of sanitizer. It also scuttles out the nonfilterable residue left by perspiration, oils, and hairsprays.

Others in the industry, however, advise that using a good skimmer, combined with draining, scrubbing, and refilling the spa or tub three or four times a year, is ultimately just as effective, as well as a healthier and less expensive method.

Water chemistry in a spa or hot tub refers to the balancing of several factors critical to health and safety. If the water chemistry changes and the water is not brought back into proper balance, damage to equipment can result. A water imbalance may also pose a risk to bathers, either directly (by irritating skin as chloramines start to form) or indirectly (by reducing the effectiveness of sanitizers).

The *pH*, or potential hydrogen, of spa or tub water should be measured at least three times each week—daily, if you soak often. It tells you where the water is on the acidity/alkalinity scale. On a logarithmic scale of 0 (total acidity) to 14 (total alkalinity), the safe, recommended pH range for either a spa or hot tub is 7.2 to 7.6.

If the pH falls lower (towards the acidic end), it can ruin your support equipment in a hurry—by etching it away—as well as pit the plaster on a concrete spa and cause eyes and skin to sting and burn.

An abnormally high pH (towards the alkaline end) can result in cloudy water that requires extra amounts of sanitizer, while reducing its effectiveness. Worse, the condition promotes *scaling*, the accumulation of calcium deposits on equipment. Since these deposits form most heavily where temperature is hottest, heaters are especially susceptible. An electric heater coil encrusted with scale can require three times more electricity than a normal unit to deliver the necessary heat to spa water.

Commonly sold by simpler product names, soda ash or sodium bicarbonate are used to raise the pH, muriatic acid or sodium bisulfate to lower it. A test kit (explained below) that shows acid and alkalai demand helps you to determine how much of either acid or alkalai to add to the water.

Total alkalinity should be tested once a week. The chemicals mentioned above can help raise or reduce the level of total alkalinity, which should stay between 80 and 140 parts per million. This range guards against formation of *excessive calcium carbonate*, which causes the scaling described above. Maintaining the proper total alkalinity also prevents the pH from rapidly fluctuating, which, in turn, makes a sanitizer like chlorine (which is very pH sensitive) more effective.

Calcium hardness, another critical factor in the spa or tub's water balance, is already familiar to anyone who has hard water. If the level becomes too high, calcium hardness disrupts the proper water chemistry. If, on the other hand, it falls too low (if the water is soft), corrosion can result. *Never* fill your tub or spa from a water supply treated by a water softener.

Test the water to maintain calcium hardness at between 150 and 400 parts per million. If the measurement is much higher than this range, it's usually time to drain the spa or tub and replace the water (as a rule, every two to four months). If the reading is too low, raise calcium hardness by adding calcium chloride.

Chemicals and Kits

Your spa or tub dealer will guide you to specific product lines of spa-care chemicals, which include test kits to make the measurements described above.

All good product lines will work on any spa or tub. However, each has been formulated as a coordinated system—if you use one chemical from a certain product line, you should use all the others in the same line. Each has its own set of instructions, some easier to follow than others. Go over them carefully, asking your dealer to clear up whatever you don't completely understand. Then, following the manufacturer's instructions, your dealer's advice, and your own soaking habits, draw up a maintenance schedule.

For sanitation, you'll find both chlorine and bromine available. Also, you'll need a kit that tests the water for its pH, total alkalinity, free chlorine or bromine, and calcium hardness. Purchase other chemicals—to raise or lower the pH, or adjust the calcium hardness—as necessary.

The key to clean, sparkling, trouble-free water is frequent testing, and this requires a good kit (see page 32 for an illustration of two types). Test kits vary; look into all options until you find the type that works best for you.

With some kits, you test the water by adding a reagent, in liquid or tablet form, to a precise amount of spa water contained in a device called a test block; comparing the color variations that result with those shown on the test block itself tells you what chemicals are needed. Other kits use strips, like litmus paper, that change color when dipped into spa water. Again, the resulting hue is compared with a printed chart for interpretation.

Either system is fine, as long as you can measure available or free sanitizer, pH, total alkalinity, and

Troubleshooting a Spa or Hot Tub

Even the most carefully maintained spa or tub will experience some kind of problem. Here's how to cure some common ones.

Cloudy water may indicate several different problems. Check that your filtration system works properly and runs often enough (2 hours daily is adequate for most small, well-maintained spas). Also check for a dirty filter.

A high pH over 7.6 can also cause clouding. Treat the water to bring down the pH.

Strong doses of chemicals and a high proportion of dissolved solids left in the water after heavy use can eventually make it cloudy. You'll have to drain the spa and refill it.

Scale sometimes leaves rough deposits on spa walls, filter, and heater, damaging the equipment and reducing its effectiveness. The underlying problem is too much dissolved calcium in the water. In the spa's hot water conditions, calcium becomes unstable, precipitating as rough calcium carbonate. The cure is to keep the pH within the correct range of 7.4 to 7.6 and to keep a regular check on total alkalinity and calcium hardness.

Irritation to eyes and skin may occur if the pH is too low or too high; sometimes chlorine or bromine is the culprit. If chlorine combines with nitrogen from perspiration or cosmetics, it forms chloramines; these give off a chlorine odor and irritate eyes. Bromine forms bromamines, equally irritating but odorless.

One remedy is to shock the water, following the water chemical manufacturer's directions explicitly. This oxidizes the chloramines or bromamines. Or, drain, clean, and refill the spa, and treat the water.

Foaming, which results from the combined effects of agitated water and traces of shampoo, lotions, or cosmetics, appears fairly often. Special antifoam products are available to eliminate the foam.

Colored water and stains indicate metals in the water. The copper components in the circulation system may release small particles under certain conditions—high velocity, low pH, low total alkalinity, or low calcium hardness. These particles can turn the water green. Other metals in the water itself may leave stains on the spa surface.

Water-care companies offer products to deal with removing metals from the water. Or you may want to change the spa water.

No chlorine or bromine reading when you test can simply mean that there *is* no free, or residual, amount in the water—or that a heavy demand for sanitizing by bacteria and organic matter has used up all the chemical you added last time. If algae is present, it sometimes consumes much of the chlorine or bromine. Simply add the necessary amount of sanitizer. Also, check your maintenance schedule—it may be time to change the water.

Be aware, though, that a very high chlorine level can bleach the color out of the reagent, making it look as if no sanitizer is present when there is actually too much. To resolve the problem of excessive sanitizer, run the blower and hydrojets for 5 to 10 minutes. Then test the water again to see if the level has dropped.

Algae can usually be prevented with regular maintenance and the strict use of a cover between soaks. To get rid of algae, chlorinate; or, drain, clean, and refill the spa.

Tests for Water Chemistry

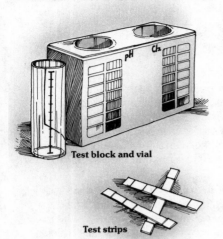

Test block and vial

Test strips

calcium hardness quickly and accurately. Remember with a test block to measure the water and reagent very carefully. Also remember when testing pH that the phenol red scale generally used runs only from 6.8 to 8.4; if your spa water tests out at the bottom or top of the color range, the water may be even more acid or alkaline than the numbers indicate.

Some dealers are now setting up small laboratories that can analyze their customers' spa or tub water. You test and correct your spa or tub water on a regular basis for a month, then bring a sample to the dealer for analysis and specific recommendations.

You can also buy a meter that attaches to your spa and measures the pH and sanitizer levels; just dip the meter into the water and the pertinent numbers are displayed in liquid crystal.

For problems beyond routine maintenance, there are products that control foaming, clarify water, clean the filter or spa surface, freshen or even perfume the water, and polish or wax the spa surface after periodic draining and cleaning.

Weekly and Periodic Cleaning

In addition to the maintenance described above, make sure your schedule includes periodic cleaning and checking. Once a week, empty the skimmer basket of any collected leaves or other debris. At the same time, check the filter's pressure gauge (if it has one); this will indicate whether the filter needs cleaning.

With average use of a spa or hot tub, the filter will need cleaning only every 4 to 6 weeks. (In the case of some portables, you'll have to wait until you're ready to drain the spa.) Most cartridge filters can be cleaned with a garden hose fitted with a pressure nozzle, although water-care companies also sell special cleansers.

Every two to four months, plan to drain and clean the spa or hot tub. This is necessary because of the natural increase of total dissolved solids over time. These particles, which can't be filtered out, make the water less responsive to chemicals and, as a result, less safe for you and for the spa or tub.

If you have a tub, do not let it stand empty of water for more than a day or two. Also, be careful of draining an in-ground spa at times when the ground is very wet—the hydrostatic pressure can pop the spa right out of the ground.

Clean the spa or tub surface with a mild, nonabrasive detergent or with a special cleanser from a water-care product line. Use a sponge, soft cloth, or very soft brush. Rinse thoroughly. Then, if you wish, you can polish a spa's surface or, if it's made of gelcoat or certain plastics, wax it to a sheen.

This is also a good time to lubricate gaskets and O-rings with specified products. After the last rinsing, refill the spa or tub with water. Then, test the water and make all the adjustments necessary to bring the water to its proper chemistry.

Mechanical Care

Generally, good water maintenance is the best overall protection against mechanical failures in a spa or tub.

Run the pump for at least 2 hours daily. Check and clean its hair/lint basket weekly or bimonthly, depending on how much use the spa gets.

The filter needs regular checks, as well as periodic cleaning. Have the heater checked annually for corrosion or scale damage. If you have a gas heater, be particularly cautious about lighting the pilot light or making any adjustments; follow the manufacturer's directions, printed on the heater, to the letter.

Give all equipment proper housing to ensure trouble-free service. For spas and tubs other than portables, be sure to allow for good ventilation on all sides and adequate protection from water, dirt, and the elements. A roof overhead and a floor raised above decking or concrete will help prolong the life of the equipment.

When you clean and drain the tub or spa, check pipe joints for leaks. Using the cover faithfully between soaks indirectly protects equipment by keeping out leaves and other debris, which could clog the filter, and by guarding against cold air, which could shorten the heater's lifespan.

Safety with Chemicals

Potentially quite hazardous, spa chemicals must be handled with great caution. Read labels carefully and follow directions explicitly. Inaccurate measurement of chemicals is the leading reason for serious water chemistry problems other than those caused by plain neglect.

Store chemicals well out of the reach of children, preferably behind locked doors. Keep them in a cool, dry, and well-ventilated location. Don't store them in the cabinet of a portable spa or in the equipment shed of an in-ground spa. Many of these chemicals are quite caustic— they can ruin wiring and controls if they stand a few inches away. Cover all containers when they're not being used and never interchange caps between two containers.

Measure accurately, never using more than the amount specified on the label (often, the container cap serves as a measuring cup). Unless label directions tell you otherwise, be careful never to mix chemicals, as this could result in a dangerous reaction. Instead, add different chemicals separately. For the same reason, you should never add water to a chemical, but add the chemical to the water.

Ideas for Sites & Settings

- **Spas & hot tubs**
- **Home saunas**
- **Finding space**
- **Designing for privacy**
- **Decks & landscaping**
- **Entertainment areas**

Besides offering a refreshing experience, a spa, hot tub, or sauna makes a dramatic impact on any home environment. Set a spa in the back yard, for example, and it immediately becomes the focus of attention, changing the appearance of everything around it. Place it on a deck and it becomes the center of an entertainment area.

Good spa, tub, or sauna design, together with thoughtful landscaping (or, sometimes, architecture), are essentials for new installations that both complement their surroundings and fit their owners' way of life. In this chapter, we present a selection of such good designs, photographed in color, for your inspiration.

Whatever you choose to surround your spa, hot tub, or sauna—redwood, tile, shrubbery, a canopy of sky—can add special enhancement. Look at the dozens of ideas shown in the photographs—you're sure to find some that you can apply to your own situation.

Protected by a glass windscreen, this spa has a panoramic view of thickly forested slopes. Design: Jerry L. Smania.

Japanese-style tub house nestles in a quiet corner of garden near end of koi pond (see plan below). Except for ¼ by 2-inch pine lattice, which conceals support equipment, tub house construction is cedar throughout. Translucent fiberglass windows, resembling shoji screens, are hinged at top; owners prop them open for fresh air and view of garden. Design: Donn Foster and Paul Bickler.

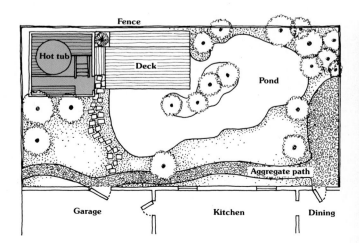

If you have a large lot . . .

A Japanese Hot-tub House for Privacy and Solitude

In Japan, the wooden hot tub traditionally has been a retreat for relaxing the mind rather than a bath for cleansing the body. Separated from the main living quarters, it was housed in a simple structure that shielded it from curious eyes. Only the immediate family and honored guests partook in the hot bath ritual, which often included tea drinking and a leisurely stroll through the garden.

Today, many Western homeowners with outdoor space to spare have adapted this Eastern idea, some constructing an entire garden in classical Japanese style. Shown here are two fine examples of the Japanese hot-tub house, American-style.

Cedar tub rests on a concrete pad. Entering tub house, owners step down to disrobing area, then climb short ladder to platform surrounding most of tub.

Half-sunken redwood tub *occupies windowed corner of room. Entire garden house, including hot tub, exercise area, shower, and sauna (see plan below), was designed and built as a single project.*

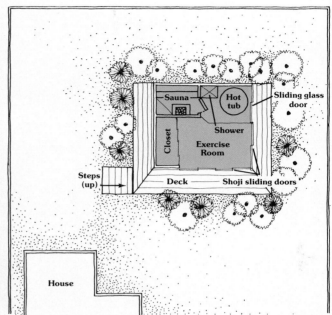

Hot-tub house *sits behind and slightly uphill of main house. Even on foggy days, owners enjoy a hot soak with shoji screens open. On clear days ". . . the view is magnificent, especially when we enjoy it from the tub." Design: Dolphin Woodworks and Maroto Imai.*

Sites & Settings **35**

Just half the length
of an average lap pool

Swim Spa Offers a Vigorous Workout

This large spa, called a swim spa, provides either a vigorous workout or a leisurely swim, depending on how you adjust the oversize jets at the head of the spa. For a workout, you turn up the jets and swim against the current they generate. Or you can turn them off, raise the temperature of the water, and invite the neighbors in for a soak.

Swim spas are typically between 13½ and 15 feet in length. Some have removable partitions that allow you to keep the water at one end hot enough for soaking, the water at the end with the swim jets at a more comfortable workout temperature.

Size doesn't matter. One of the installations shown on this page is sunk into the ground of a modest-size patio. The other is part of a grand complex of decks, steps, and benches. Both are near the house, which means foot traffic can move freely from indoors to outdoors.

Whether for an intimate group or a large gathering, whether people are steaming in the water or standing around the tub's edge, the outdoor hot bath is a natural nucleus for socializing.

Part of a master bedroom addition, this swim spa was brought indoors by extending existing roof with radially arranged glass and by adding extensive glazing to take advantage of the view. Spa, made of fiberglass, was tiled in place. A black slate deck surrounds spa. Installation includes a hot tub for easing tired muscles after a workout in swim spa. Design: S. Robert Politzer.

An entertainment extension
for the house

A Socializing Area for Family and Friends

It's bound to happen! Desiring your place in the sun, you site your spa or hot tub outdoors, and in no time at all it becomes more than just a watering spot. You and your family may use it strictly for soaking, but when friends come over it becomes a gathering place, a full-blown entertainment center.

Size doesn't matter. One of the installations shown on this page is sunk into the ground of a modest-size patio. The other is part of a grand complex of decks, steps, and benches. Both are near the house, which means foot traffic can move freely from indoors to outdoors.

Whether for an intimate group or a large gathering, whether people are steaming in the water or standing around the tub's edge, the outdoor hot bath is a natural nucleus for socializing.

Company gathers around *commodious redwood tub. Its interior benches are located to take advantage of 10 jets arranged in pairs. Gas-fired heater, pump, and filter are housed under deck, close to tub. Design: Roger Somers.*

Near entertaining area, *redwood hot tub is set below grade in a concrete vault sunk in brick patio floor. A course of ceramic tile—held by a special epoxy adhesive—is inset flush with the redwood around tub's top. Tub's support equipment is located nearby in a small brick structure that looks like a decorative wall. Design: Malibu Spa.*

Outdoors, but very close by

Just a Step Away from the House

Locating a spa or tub close to the house not only minimizes the chilling effects of cool evening air after a hot soak but also makes the spa or tub a natural extension of the nearby rooms. Moreover, because of its proximity, the house can help to provide privacy and wind control without the need for screens or fences.

The three examples shown here vary in style and setting, but they do share one feature: all are a hop, skip, and a jump away from the warmth, privacy, and convenience of the house.

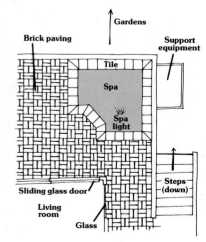

Sharing a magnificent view with a glassed-in living room, spa is less than 10 feet from house, but, thanks to large used-brick patio that surrounds it, it's a focal point for outdoor entertaining. Both the brick and the red tile coping around spa echo Spanish-style roof below. Spa is a ceramic-tiled, in-ground unit; its support equipment is housed below in garden. Design: Locksin Thompson, Blackthorne Hot Tubs.

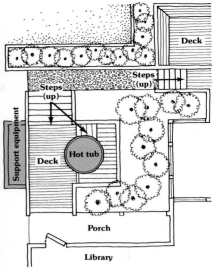

Accessible to library, *redwood tub nestles in deck tucked into a small side yard (see plan above). Owners make year-round use of tub, which has a fine view and is protected from breezes by house and plantings. Design: Bennett, Johnson, Slenes, and Smith.*

Opening off family room, *two-level cedar deck surrounds redwood tub resting on a 4-inch concrete slab. Shingled wall behind tub provides privacy and helps hide support equipment (see plan at left). Semicircular wooden tub covers stand against wall. Design: Robert C. and Janet Slenes.*

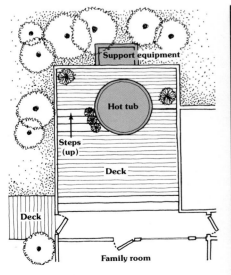

You can build them in
or just plug them in

Portables Adapt to Changing Circumstances and Sites

Because portable spas house all their equipment beneath their skirts, they're wonderfully flexible in how they can be used. For the renter or transient homeowner, a portable's small footprint and plug-in convenience are important. But for those who are more permanently settled, most portables can be hard-wired to 220 volts for faster heating and built in for greater convenience and a more attractive appearance.

The examples on these pages range from a portable with just a little embellishment to one that has been completely built in.

Canopy overhead and extension to the side lend a feeling of permanence to this portable spa. Ceramic tile on extension carries out color of spa and gives bathers a place for towels and refreshments. Chemicals can be isolated in cabinet beneath, where their caustic vapors won't harm spa equipment. Trellis creates an arbor effect, contributing shade and privacy. Design: East Bay Builders.

Fit into a snug corner, this portable is just as it came from showroom floor. Spa's strong, solid color, which matches dark green of house trim, adds to its appeal and makes it look at home. Attractive redwood fence, with its alternating panels of wide vertical boards and lattice work, provides color and texture, as well as privacy and shelter from wind.

Step up to this graceful deck and entertainment area, complete with a self-contained spa. Although it's no longer strictly portable, owners chose this type over an in-ground spa because of its more economical purchase price and lower operating costs. Access to spa's skid pack (containing support equipment) is through small, hinged door. Design: Gary Marsh, All Decked Out.

Building a world
all your own

Spas with a Sense of Privacy

For many owners, a hot soak offers a relaxing escape from the crowds, noise, and stress of daily life. Essential to this peace of mind is an intimate setting that shuts out the world. Sometimes, creating a symbolic retreat, like the gazebo on this page, is enough. For greater outdoor privacy, nothing is more effective than a stone wall, particularly when it adds as much to the visual environment as the flagstone example shown on the opposite page.

Bright with Victorian charm, custom-made gazebo establishes visual boundaries for spa and gives it an intimacy otherwise impossible to achieve in large, irregularly shaped back yard. It also provides privacy in a neighborhood with two-story houses, yet doesn't sacrifice feeling of being outdoors. Gazebo was built in modules, then bolted together on site. Gazebo design: Charles Lemmonier, Gazebo Nostalgia.

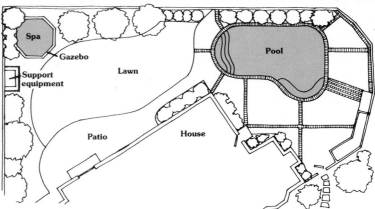

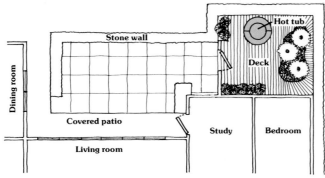

Small, enclosed garden extends house's Mediterranean architectural theme. Tub, sited just inside arched doorway in stone wall, is accessible by a short stroll through patio. Housing for support equipment is on other side of wall. Design: Howdy King.

Labels on plan: Stone wall · Dining room · Covered patio · Living room · Hot tub · Deck · Study · Bedroom

The lean look

Keeping a Low Profile

Though they may look great on the showroom floor, spas and hot tubs need a lot of camouflage when you get them home. Otherwise, your spa may look like a giant dog dish or your tub like a rain barrel. Also, the higher they are placed in the deck, the more difficult it is to get in and out.

One of the best solutions is to sink the spa or tub down into the deck and to keep the decking itself low. This takes some careful planning, but the results are worth it.

Modest-size redwood deck, measuring only 10 by 14 feet, was designed to hold hot tub and to fit into a small side yard off guest bedroom and bath. Redwood tub has eight jets and three benches at different levels. Turned-wood grabposts help tubbers get in and out of water easily. Design: Donald G. Boos.

Concrete patio was already there; so was Japanese black pine (at left). Owners wanted to keep both, but they also preferred a more natural look—and they desired a hot tub. The answer was to put a redwood tub on a new concrete pad and a redwood deck right over the old concrete, leaving an opening in deck for pine. And while they were at it, they added benches and a table for outdoor living. Design: Ed Hoiland.

Echoing octagonal shape *of spa it surrounds, this deck is about 18 inches higher than the water, making spa the natural focal point and providing seating for sunworshippers. Low rail helps to solve privacy problems. To make cleanup easier, add a spot where leaves and other debris accumulating on lower deck can be swept out.*

Circular redwood tub *shown above sits entirely beneath ground-level deck. Tub was wrapped in several layers of tar paper, sealed with asphalt, then buried in soil to within 10 inches of its rim. Its plumbing and wiring—boxed in a wooden "tube"— run for 30 feet under the deck to support equipment adjoining house. Design: Ed Stiles.*

If you want to be bold

Spas and Tubs Create a Focal Point in the Garden

When you want to make a strong statement, you can let a spa or hot tub create a striking focal point in your landscape. First you site the spa or tub where it will serve your needs best; then you structure a total environment around it, using decking and plants.

Among the many design tricks you can use to focus attention on the spa or tub are radial decking patterns, changes in scale or level, the use of contours and curves, and dense plantings that screen out distractions and provide vivid color.

Narrow strip garden shown above runs width of back lot and is bounded by privacy wall and concrete patio. Owners wanted an outdoor hot bath but were reluctant to give up too much of the garden. The solution was an eye-catching, wooden tub with compact deck and stairs. Support equipment is behind metal gate at far right. Design: California Redwood Spa.

Tight space behind house became a total outdoor environment when spa was made focal point. Sunburst-pattern decking and steps emphasize its shape. Design: Robert Clay.

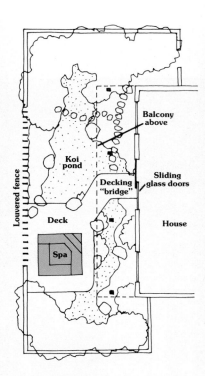

Tranquil glade *is created in this narrow back yard by careful siting of spa and use of dense landscaping. Shallow, free-form koi pond surrounds redwood deck and tiled fiberglass spa, making them appear to float. Eight-inch-wide vertical copper louvers in fence open for ventilation, close up with touch of a switch for privacy and security. Design: Pacific Water Works and Rob Newman.*

Enjoying the outdoors inside

Spa and Sunspace— a Winning Combination

Spas and sunspaces go together naturally, particularly in cooler climates. The indoor spa can be enjoyed even in the coldest weather, and the wide expanse of glass opens the room to the outside. Besides keeping down the operating costs of the spa, a well-ventilated sunspace is the best indoor location for dealing with the heat and humidity produced by the spa.

Scaled-down garden, *extensive use of glass, and repetition of color and line integrate carefully landscaped back yard with indoor spa room. Deciduous vines growing on trellis outside will help shade spa in summer and bring outdoors closer to bathers. Thermal storage in floor keeps room warm even after sun has gone down. Design: Tim Magee, Rainshadow.*

For both a swim and a soak

Spa and Pool Share Single Setting

At home in a natural setting of giant ferns and lush foliage, poolside gunite spa has feel of a small, upstream tributary. But its location just a few steps from the house makes it a good deal more practical. Irregular flagstones line edge of pool, creating spa spillway and dividing spa from pool. Design: Jack Buktenica.

Since both a pool and a spa can be built with the same construction techniques and operated with the same equipment, they often appear together. The pool provides ample space to swim and play, and the spa offers hydrojets, hotter water, and a more intimate setting. The savings is in building them at the same time; the challenge is in creating an integrated design.

In the installation below, it's hard to tell where the spa ends and the pool begins. A narrow spillway at the far end of the spa in the foreground gives it away.

Seclusion, privacy,
and informality

Natural
Hot Tubs
in Natural
Settings

Maybe it's a hot tub's unfinished wood that literally says "outdoors." Maybe it's the harmonious round form. Maybe it's the sparkling water. But, somehow, a tub looks right in a setting of trees, boulders, and other wild things.

As evidenced by the four varied installations shown on these two pages, a hot tub harmonizes with almost any natural setting. One rests in a thicket of aspens near a rushing creek; another fits into a rocky hillside; another tucks into a cluster of redwood trees; yet another nestles in a grove of oaks.

Countryside cedar hot tub is sited to take full advantage of a wooded setting. Tub rests in a below-grade insulated room, which protects it in freezing weather. Thermostat-controlled pump circulates water automatically if water temperature falls below 55°F/13°C. Design: Steve Moeller.

Hot tub family fun is in a natural setting where privacy is no problem (installation is between house and rocky hillside). Like the massive rocks, redwood deck is at several levels, making benches unnecessary. Tub rests on a concrete slab. Design: Marla Simpson.

Redwood grove encloses shallow redwood tub, which has no benches inside. Soakers sit on a duckboard false floor that covers an air-bubbler ring. Resting on a concrete slab over chine joists, tub has, at rear, a shelf for seating or for towels. Heater, pump, and filter are located 40 feet away, near house.

Freestanding redwood tub is situated near property line under large oak tree. Towels hang on wooden pegs in fence; redwood rounds lead from tub to rear deck of house. Support equipment is located 30 feet away in a small shed.

Finding that unused corner

Hot Tub and Spa That Take Advantage of Little-used Space

Since most spas and hot tubs are added to existing homesites, finding space for them can be a major problem. The installation shown on this page was tucked into one end of a small deck area, often all the space available in an urban environment. Though the home shown on the opposite page is waterfront property, it, too, offered no yard. Yet the owner found a clever way to take advantage of the available space.

Tight space off master bedroom was seldom used by owners of hillside home until they installed a redwood hot tub. Bedroom wall and small fence (see plan) give soakers privacy and wind protection. Support equipment is housed behind fence in enclosed cabinet insulated against freezing temperatures. Design: Colorado Hot Tub Co.

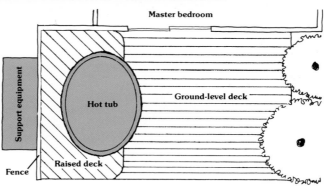

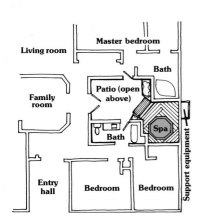

Converging roof lines *open patio to outside but minimize exposure to weather. Horizontal redwood siding in spa area visually separates space from adjoining patio. Doorway in center leads to master bedroom; kitchen and family room are through French doors on left.*

Japanese motif characterizes this hot water retreat, formerly an awkward small space. Flanked by bedrooms and hallways, it's centrally located, yet very private. Shoji screens overhead conceal operable skylights. Simulated-marble acrylic spa is set in sand; support equipment is housed outside. Because patio off spa room is open to outside, heat and humidity aren't a problem. Design: Keith Wallach.

Only the materials have changed

Drawing On Eastern Tradition

Hot water bathing has long been a Japanese tradition, important enough to warrant separate bath houses for its exclusive enjoyment (see pages 34 and 35).

Like many Japanese customs, the form of the bath is prescribed, and the intent is specific—not to wash the body but to relax it and lift the soul. You can derive these same benefits from a hot bath, whether you use the traditional wood ofuro, a tiled tub, or a thermoplastic spa.

Ceramic tile stands in for wood in American version of Japanese bath, but simplicity is still the theme. Conventionally plumbed 4 by 6-foot spa is covered with cedar panels when not in use. Steam-glazed windows soften garden view. Design: Joseph Esherick.

Classic Japanese ofuro has been rendered in sleek, modern lines. No hydrojets, blowers, or lights here—just a hot water soak for one. Wood tub, banded with brass, is filled directly from water heater through an oversize brass pipe. Design: Arthur Hanna.

Following Japanese custom, bathers lather, scrub down, and rinse under shower, then step into tub for a long soak. Spa has a permanently mounted faucet for adding water but is maintained like other spas. Vertical-grain fir trim contrasts with vivid blue ceramic tile. Design: Glen Wm. Jarvis.

Spa Plus Sauna Equal Home Health Center

Some people prefer wet heat. Some prefer dry heat. Then there are those who like both. The answer: A home health center that includes a spa (or hot tub) for simmering and a sauna for baking.

But doesn't all that equipment take a lot of room? Not as much as you might think. One of the installations shown on these two pages went together during contruction of a new house. But the other two were conversions of existing space; one had been a basement workshop, the other a spare bedroom.

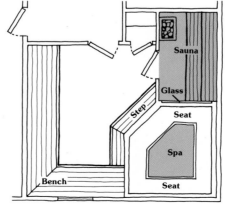

Home health center containing spa, sauna, storage, and benches (see plan) was converted from a spare bedroom. Modest-size 5 by 6-foot sauna seems more spacious because of its thermal window wall and door. Spa room has a fan and two outside-opening windows to exhaust moisture-laden air. Spa support equipment is housed below benches. Design: David A. Konsmo.

Spa/sauna room, *converted from a former basement-level workshop, allows owners to bring the health club home. Floor of spa room (see far right) is covered with indoor-outdoor carpeting; walls and ceiling are redwood sealed with a clear urethane finish to resist moisture. Wood grating edges spa, covering drain that carries off splashed water. Sauna has two wider-than-average benches, one 24 inches above the floor, the other 44 inches high. Design: David A. Konsmo.*

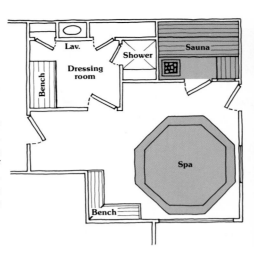

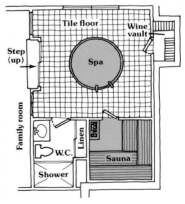

Spacious soaking room *(as viewed from sauna) has one window wall looking out on a deck. Redwood hot tub, below floor level, rests on redwood sills that are anchored to concrete blocks atop a concrete slab sloped for drainage. This home health center has not only a bathroom and shower, but also a wine vault. Design: Glen A. Patterson.*

Sites & Settings **57**

If you have space to spare . . .

Outdoor Saunas That Stand Alone

A freestanding outdoor sauna does require space. It also requires extra runs of plumbing and either electrical wiring or gas lines. But many sauna enthusiasts wouldn't have their sweat bath any other way.

"When I step out of the sauna I like to be outside, not inside," stated one owner.

Said another: "We had a swimming pool, so putting the sauna near it seemed like a good idea."

The sauna/swimming pool idea *is* a good one. Immediately after leaving the heated sauna, you can plunge into cool water. Both of the sauna houses shown on pages 60–61 are situated adjacent to swimming pools.

Rustic, freestanding sauna *opens to forest on one side, to dressing room and shower on other side. Exterior is shingled with hand-split shakes; interior is 1 by 8 cedar panels. Wood-burning brick stove has a counterbalanced metal hood—you raise it to lay the fire, then fit it snugly over firebox for heat buildup. Combustion air is drawn from outside. Design: Arch W. Diack.*

Owner-built sauna *has sturdy base of 4 by 4s resting on a concrete patio between house and swimming pool. Plywood exterior, with decorative battens and cupola, is painted in Wisconsin-barn style; roof is shingled. Interior paneling is 1 by 4-inch cedar. Floor space of approximately 40 square feet (height is 7 feet) accommodates six adults on two benches. Heater is 7.5-kilowatt electric unit. Design: James Dearborn.*

...saunas that stand alone

Sturdy sauna house, *looking like a permanent part of forest, rests on a concrete-pier foundation with a retaining wall at back slope. Siding (1 by 6-inch boards, 1 by 2-inch battens) is untreated rough fir, which adds to natural appearance of structure. Asphalt shingles cover roof. Windows bring light inside, yet are high enough for privacy. Situated near swimming pool, sauna house also serves as a dressing room, as shown in plan below.*

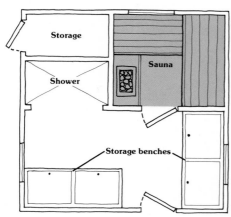

Sauna house, *measuring 6 by 9 feet (with 7-foot ceiling), is paneled in finished fir and has a wood-burning stove. Benches are staggered to let three people stretch out, half a dozen sit. As shown in plan at far left, outer room has a shower, benches for relaxing, and storage for towels, swimming pool accessories, and stove wood.*

Custom-built sauna house—*framed by a backdrop of trees—rests on a concrete foundation at one end of swimming pool. Siding is ⅝-inch resawn fir panels stained gray; roof is cedar shingles. See plan and interior view below.*

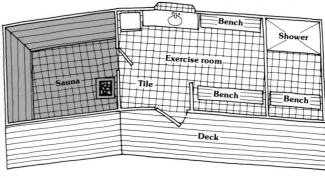

Western red cedar *lines walls and ceiling; two-level benches are Alaskan yellow cedar. The 8 by 10-foot interior (with 7-foot ceiling) is heated by a 9-kilowatt electric stove. Ceramic tile on floor extends into exercise room. Instruments on far wall of sauna room are sand timer and thermometer. Design: Finska Sauna.*

When space is at a premium

Squeezing in the Small-space Sauna

As hopeless as the small-space problem may sometimes seem, don't despair. The owners of the saunas shown on these two pages did a remarkable job of finding a practical answer.

For sheer imagination—and inspiration—look closely at the unorthodox sauna and spa combination on this page. To locate the sauna shown on the opposite page, the owners converted an unused portion of a service porch/laundry area.

Fold-out sauna bench in "down" position rests on rear half of circular spa (its rim is teak) in a tiny room whose walls are half paneled with wood, half tiled. As shown in plan at right, 6-kilowatt electric heater is recessed into wall at end of bench. Reflecting tiles around stove help heat room. Design: Douglas R. Zuberbuhler.

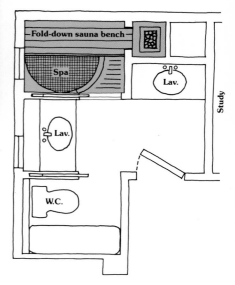

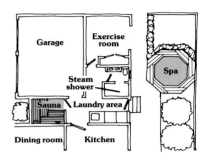

Though spacious in feel, *this cedar sauna is small enough to make an electric heater practical. Bench heights and widths were carefully calculated to make maximum number of people comfortable in both seated and prone positions; note how supports for upper benches were angled back toward wall to create more space. On wall at left is a cover that lifts out to reveal electrical service panel for house, an apparatus that had to be accommodated. Design: John Kolkka, Finnish-American Sauna.*

Tucked into unused space *between garage and kitchen/dining area, sauna is convenient to large steam shower, exercise room, and spa. Open shelves hold towels and stereo equipment; speakers are built in under benches inside sauna.*

A Look at Home Saunas

- **The Finnish sauna**
- **Design ideas**
- **Choosing a stove**
- **How to take a sauna**
- **Maintenance**

Known to Finns as the *sauna,* dry-heat bathing is a 2,000-year-old custom of many cultures that has warmed its way into American homes with surprising speed. Increasingly, Americans are discovering what Europeans have known all along—that the dry-heat bath is one of life's most physically and mentally refreshing experiences.

Whether you're planning to build or buy a sauna, you'll benefit from the information in this chapter. Here you'll learn what to look for in sauna room construction, stoves, accessories, and custom touches. You'll also find help in planning the sauna's location, indoors or outdoors.

To enhance your enjoyment of Finland's favorite way to relax, we've included a little history, as well as directions on how to take a sauna. Be sure to allow plenty of time for your sauna— nothing can equal the traditional Finnish experience.

A burst of steam, *or lőyly, is produced by splashing a ladle of water on hot sauna rocks.*

An early sauna—from an 18th century etching by Giuseppe Acerbi.

If you've ever stretched out lazily on a bench in the heat of a 195°F/91°C room long enough to perspire freely from every pore in your body—and if you've ever enjoyed the skin-tingling sensation of plunging into cool water (or a snowbank) afterward—you've known the pleasure of a Finnish sauna.

Sauna (say "*sow*-na"—*sow* as in cow; "*saw*-na" if you prefer the American pronunciation) is the Finnish art of perspiration bathing. And, though the sweat bath has been with us for better than 2,000 years (the Greeks, Romans, Russians, Slavs, Turks, Africans, Germans, Eskimos, Irish, Mexicans, Mayans, and North American Indians all have practiced or still do practice it in one form or another), it is the Finns whom Americans have to thank for its growing popularity here.

The Sauna Experience

The sauna is an insulated wooden room heated from 160° to 195°F/ 71° to 91°C (sometimes even higher) that provides a restorative environment for the body. Its heat, usually very dry with less than 30 percent humidity, deep cleanses the skin through induced perspiration, stimulates circulation, and reduces muscular tension.

"Going to sauna" involves a cycle, repeated once or twice, that begins with a brief exposure to the sauna's intense heat, followed by gradual or rapid cooling with a shower, plunge into cool water, or—if you are a hardy sauna enthusiast—roll in the snow; and lastly, a period of quiet rest.

But the sauna experience is different for everyone because no two saunas are the same, and no two people respond to heat in the same way. You'll find as many variations on the sauna ritual—temperature, degree of humidity, length of stay, method of cooling, and so on—as you'll find sauna enthusiasts.

Health Benefits

"If spirits, tar, and the sauna can avail nothing, then there is no cure," goes an old Finnish saying, and even today some sauna enthusiasts are inclined to agree. The sauna has been attributed with healing everything from common colds to broken bones, although little medical research or evidence exists to support such claims.

Almost everyone agrees that the sauna makes you feel good. The combination of free perspiration, rapid cooling, and rest stimulates circulation to rid the body of impurities through the skin and liver, reduces muscular and nervous tension, and heightens mental awareness.

After strenuous workouts athletes often use the sauna to relax tired muscles. Some doctors prescribe it for patients with arthritis or rheumatism because the sauna's heat temporarily eases tension in the joints and muscles. It also has been known to temporarily relieve symptoms of colds, sinus congestion, and other minor respiratory ailments or allergies; poor circulation; tension headache; and acne (heat softens the oil plugs that block skin pores).

What the sauna does not do, as some have claimed, is help you lose weight permanently (without dieting). While it's true you'll weigh less after a sauna, the loss is primarily in water—little fat is burned.

The Finnish Ritual

In Finland, the sauna is as beloved an institution as the baseball season in America. Found wherever Finns live, from modern urban high-rises to backcountry farms, saunas even outnumber automobiles in Finland. And, for every sauna in the country, there seems to be a traditional proverb, such as "No Finn without his sauna," or "Sauna makes a woman most beautiful one hour after the bath." It has even been traditional practice for a Finn to build his sauna before building his house.

Not merely a source of physical renewal, the Finnish sauna is also regarded as a means of mental relaxation and quiet contemplation, as

Birch whisk in hand, a Finn crosses his snow-covered yard en route to the family sauna. The sauna is so deeply rooted in Finnish tradition that even war didn't interfere with its practice.

Home Saunas **65**

well as an activity to be shared by family and friends.

Saturday evening has customarily been reserved for the bath (though today any day of the week is suitable). After a good wood fire has heated rocks in the stove and warmed the walls and benches, family and perhaps a few neighbors gather in the soft heat of the "ripened" sauna. Children often sit on the lower benches, where it's cooler; adults usually prefer the hotter air higher up.

Within 5 to 10 minutes most bathers begin to perspire freely. Soon everyone leaves the sauna to cool off in the fresh air or in a nearby pond or stream, returning later to the friendly heat of the sauna.

Bursts of steam (*löyly*) punctuate the second visit to the sauna when one of the bathers ladles water over the hot rocks to add moisture to the air. Then, taking *vihtas* (bundles of leafy birch twigs tied together) from their pegs, bathers whisk themselves lightly from head to toe, stimulating circulation and filling the air with a delicate birch fragrance.

A brisk, scrubdown shower with soft brushes and perhaps another invigorating dip into cool water end the bath itself; but it is also traditional to prolong the ritual with a period of rest and relaxation to cool down completely and to enjoy a *saunapala* —sauna snack.

Sauna, American-style

Though the sauna arrived in America with the first Finnish immigrants in 1638, the heat bath was almost exclusively an ethnic practice until the 1950s. In fact, now and then the Finnish sauna aroused considerable suspicion among people who didn't understand why men, women, and children would sit naked together in a hot room and then jump around in the snow. Occasionally, innocent bathers walked out of the sauna into the hands of the law.

The high regard Finnish-Americans held for the sauna, however, gradually aroused the curiosity of other Americans who began to discover its invigorating benefits. Then, with the development of the electric sauna heater in Finland and Sweden in the 1930s, home saunas—easy to install and use—began to multiply.

By the 1960s sauna had become a household word, and saunas began to appear in resorts, locker rooms, and executive offices.

The Modern Sauna Complex

"Sauna" is a Finnish word that technically refers to the room where the heat bath is taken, since for hundreds of years the entire sauna was simply a one-room cabin.

With an architectural metamorphosis from cabin to complex, however, "sauna" has come to refer to the triad of rooms—shower, dressing/relaxation, and stove-room—as well as to the bathing process itself.

A One-room Climate

Most important of the three rooms is the one heated for the sauna. It's basically an insulated wooden box, usually rectangular, and simply furnished with two or three tiers of wooden benches. It is heated by a special stove designed to hold about 70 pounds (average for a family sauna) of igneous or metamorphic rocks (see "Sauna rocks," page 76), which, when heated, pass a soft, continuous heat into the room.

Properly designed and built, the sauna will provide just the right climate for an enjoyable heat bath. It should be well insulated, neither too big nor too small, correctly ventilated, and properly heated. Wood used for paneling and benches should stay pleasant to touch in a heated room, and benches should be wide enough for reclining bathers.

Design: size and shape. It's possible to have any shape or size sauna

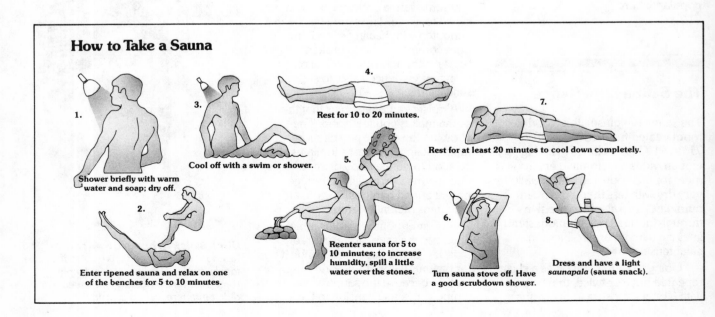

How to Take a Sauna

1. Shower briefly with warm water and soap; dry off.

2. Enter ripened sauna and relax on one of the benches for 5 to 10 minutes.

3. Cool off with a swim or shower.

4. Rest for 10 to 20 minutes.

5. Reenter sauna for 5 to 10 minutes; to increase humidity, spill a little water over the stones.

6. Turn sauna stove off. Have a good scrubdown shower.

7. Rest for at least 20 minutes to cool down completely.

8. Dress and have a light *saunapala* (sauna snack).

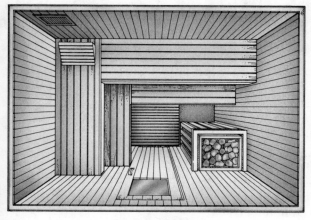

Bird's-eye View

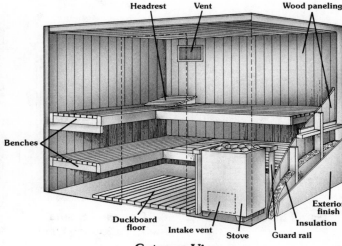

Headrest · Vent · Wood paneling

Benches

Duckboard floor · Intake vent · Stove · Guard rail · Insulation · Exterior finish

Cutaway View

The sauna is a well-insulated, ventilated, wood-paneled room heated by a special stove. It contains two levels of benches, often with a backrest or headrest; the lower level stays "cooler."

you want, but you should be aware of several rules of thumb that guide professional planners.

Size. Saunas range in size from tiny cubicles 3 by 3 by 7' high for prefabricated mini-saunas that squeeze into closets and other small spots, to rooms 12 by 16 by 9' high for public saunas that accommodate large numbers of bathers.

The size sauna you choose should depend on 1) the number of people you expect to be using the sauna at once (allow 65 cubic feet, about 2.5 cubic yards, of space for each bather); 2) the amount of space available for the sauna, and perhaps accompanying dressing room and bath; 3) arrangement of the benches (one wall dimension should be at least 6 feet long so you can lie down); 4) the size stove your budget can afford; and 5) your overall budget. Two popular sizes for family saunas are 5 by 7 by 7' high, or 6 by 6 by 7' high. Larger rooms generally require more powerful and thus more expensive stoves; extra lumber for framing, paneling, and benches; and additional batts of insulation.

Regardless of the floor dimensions, standard recommended ceiling height is 7 feet for family saunas. This lower-than-average ceiling prevents heat from rising into unused space.

Shape. By far the most popular shapes, rectangular and square saunas allow for maximum use of bench

space—an important consideration in sauna use. Octagonal, round, even wedge-shaped saunas aren't unknown, but you cannot expect their bench arrangements to offer the same flexibility.

Dressing Room and Shower

For the simple reason that the ritual involves a heating-cooling-rest process, most saunas are installed near or designed to include a dressing room and shower.

The dressing room, often the same size or larger than the sauna proper, is usually furnished with benches, a closet or pegs for clothing, a small linen closet for extra towels and accessories, and a place to put jewelry, watches, and glasses.

If your dressing room is the only place you have to cool off (and it's often the case with freestanding saunas), plan for wide benches, perhaps cushioned, so you can stretch out comfortably.

Locating Your Sauna

Few people are fortunate enough to have wooded property that opens to a placid pond or bubbling stream—the classic setting for traditional Finnish saunas. Fortunately, it's not necessary to have a picturesque setting

for your sauna. You are still free to enjoy its invigorating benefits whether you place it outdoors or in, near a swimming pool, or in a corner of the basement.

Outdoor saunas. Outdoors may be a particularly good location for your sauna if you can install it near an existing swimming pool; this way, you're only a few steps away from a plunge into cool water after you leave the hot sauna.

You also may prefer an outdoor sauna if you can tuck it into an unused corner of the yard that's made private with trees and shrubs. Include outdoor furniture or benches in your plan so you can relax in the open air between sauna visits.

Your primary consideration in erecting an outdoor sauna is the cost of plumbing, electric wiring (220-volt as well as 110-volt), or gas lines (if gas is your source of heat).

When you do install an outdoor sauna, try to situate it on level ground. Plan on privacy screens or hedges if you enjoy nude plunges into your pool.

Indoor saunas. Indoors you may have many options for locating a sauna, as well as the advantage of its convenience on wet winter days.

If the sauna is adjacent to the master bath, you also often have the

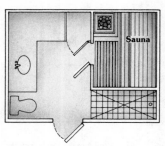
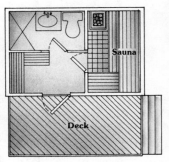
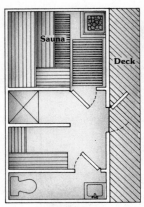
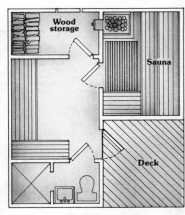

Small Indoor Sauna

Compact Sauna with Adjoining Deck

Large Sauna with Adjoining Deck

Wood-burning Sauna

Contemporary saunas, whether linked to a bathroom or located outdoors, usually include dressing room and shower; some lead to open-air sitting spots.

advantages of an existing dressing room, shower, and rest area.

Or, consider converting part of your utility room, an extra storeroom or pantry, or a basement corner into a sauna. Also consider attic space, a spare bedroom, or part of your garage. In most cases existing walls and floor can be used to simplify construction.

Your Options in Saunas

Today the home sauna buyer has a wealth of options in sauna design, construction, and materials that suit almost any taste and budget.

Prefabricated, or modular, saunas —kits that come complete with framed, insulated, and paneled walls and ceiling, benches, door, sauna stove, and hardware—are so streamlined that it's possible to snap, bolt, or lock one together in an afternoon.

You can buy a sauna kit for almost any size room indoors; and, if you want your sauna outdoors, you can purchase a kit that includes exterior roofing and siding. Some manufacturers even sell cottages that include sauna, dressing room, shower, kitchenette, and bedroom.

Most manufacturers are willing to make some custom modifications for prefabricated rooms, such as build-

ing wider benches or providing a different exterior finish.

Precut saunas also are available; using your specifications many sauna manufacturers will provide a bundle of materials (interior paneling, framing lumber, insulation batts, stove, etc.) for you to assemble. Precut saunas might be your best bet if you're handy with a hammer.

Custom-built saunas suit oddly shaped spaces and more sophisticated tastes, and usually are designed by architects or sauna builders. They offer the greatest design flexibility, but they are often more expensive than prefabricated or precut units. A custom sauna can be as traditional as a Finnish log house situated by a stream or as unorthodox as a specialized shower stall.

If you plan to build your sauna from scratch, you can purchase almost all of the materials, including stove, control panel, and hardware, from a sauna manufacturer or retail distributor.

How to Buy a Prefab Sauna

Shopping for a prefabricated (or modular) sauna is very similar to shopping for a major household appliance or automobile—you need to do a little research before buying.

You'll find only about a dozen manufacturers of prefabricated saunas in the United States. Some are large, with distributors in most metropolitan areas; others are small, one or two-person operations with sales restricted to a single region. All sell standard packages, either for indoor or outdoor installation, and a few also manufacture custom modular units to suit an architect's specifications or your own needs.

Whether standard or custom-built, prefabricated saunas usually come in easy-to-handle packages with parts numbered to coincide with step-by-step assembly instructions. The only tools you usually need to assemble one are a hammer, screwdriver, framing square and level, and perhaps a drill.

Before you choose a prefabricated sauna, read about sauna construction in the following section, "Anatomy of a Well-built Sauna." Whether a sauna is custom-built or prefabricated, certain standards exist for materials used in construction as well as for construction techniques. Knowing them will help you when you compare prefabricated units for quality of design, materials, and workmanship.

Next, visit dealers in your area, examine their display models, and ask for literature, price lists, and a copy of assembly instructions. (Don't be dazzled by slick promotional literature; some manufacturers of fine quality saunas and stoves will have only mimeographed or photocopied brochures to give you.)

Then, as you compare saunas, examine their design, materials used in construction, ease of installation, dealer warranty, and package weight. Compare the packages as well; some manufacturers include everything but the floor; others may also exclude exterior finishes, stove, or stove controls, depending on their pricing systems. (In some cases you may want to purchase the room from one manufacturer and the correct size stove from another.)

You also may find it worth your time to ask your sauna distributor to show you several saunas that have been installed longer than a year. Talk to homeowners to find out if they are satisfied with their sauna's construction as well as the performance of the stove and sauna controls.

Assembling a Prefab Sauna

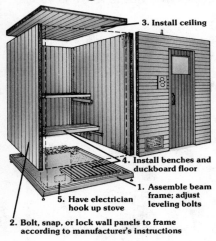

3. Install ceiling

4. Install benches and duckboard floor

1. Assemble beam frame; adjust leveling bolts

5. Have electrician hook up stove

2. Bolt, snap, or lock wall panels to frame according to manufacturer's instructions

Ask to look over the interior, too. Study the paneling to check the quality of both the wood and the construction. You can recognize clear heart redwood or cedar by the absence of knots and whitish sapwood.

Also watch out for any cracks, however miniscule, around the window or door, or where the ceiling meets the walls. Keep an eye out for any exposed sap or heads of screws or nails; these can get hot enough to cause burns.

Anatomy of a Well-built Sauna

Whether you plan to build your own sauna or buy a prefabricated or precut unit, the following information will help you understand what's important and peculiar to sauna construction, from foundation to finishing touches.

Consider a sauna addition as you would the addition of a room to your house. Like a room addition, a sauna requires an adequate foundation, proper flooring, framing, wiring, insulation, interior and exterior finishes, and furniture and decorative details that make the sauna functional and comfortable.

If you are an experienced home craftsman, you probably can build your own sauna over a period of several weekends. If not, give the job to a reliable sauna builder or a contractor with sauna-building experience; perhaps you can make arrangements to do some of the minor tasks yourself. Usually it's not difficult installing insulation, for instance, and if you don't mind the hard labor, you probably can dig foundation trenches.

If you choose to have your sauna built by a sauna specialist or contractor, do some preliminary checking. Ask to see several saunas installed by the contractor and talk to the people who own them. Base your final choice on the builder's reputation rather than on the lowest bid; he should be well-established, licensed, cooperative, financially solvent, and insured for workmen's compensation, property damage, and public liability.

If you decide to build your own sauna, you'll find helpful basic construction information in other *Sunset* building books listed on the back cover of this book.

Foundations and Floors

The type of foundation and floor your sauna needs depends on where it's located, what kind of floor surface you prefer, your climate, and the condition and slope of your property

if the sauna is to be freestanding (or attached to the existing structure).

Foundations. Indoors, where you are converting existing space into a sauna, all you may need to do initially is to put down a wood frame and subfloor over the existing floor; the existing floor serves as the foundation.

If you are building an outdoor sauna and you live in an area where the ground doesn't freeze, you can install foundation and floor at the same time by putting down a slab of concrete over sand or fine gravel (see illustrations below) that's covered with a sheet of heavy polyethylene plastic. The plastic keeps moisture from penetrating the slab.

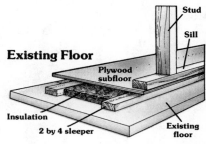

Existing Floor

Stud

Sill

Plywood subfloor

Insulation

2 by 4 sleeper

Existing floor

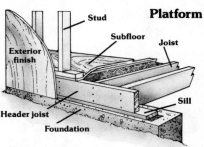

Platform

Stud

Subfloor

Joist

Exterior finish

Sill

Header joist

Foundation

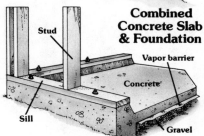

Combined Concrete Slab & Foundation

Stud

Vapor barrier

Concrete

Sill

Gravel

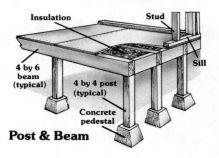

Post & Beam

Insulation

Stud

4 by 6 beam (typical)

4 by 4 post (typical)

Sill

Concrete pedestal

Where the ground does freeze, you must install a more substantial foundation of wood or masonry construction, below frost line, which will resist damage caused by frost heaving. You may also want to insulate the floor; if the foundation is of wood construction, you can place fiberglass batts between the floor joists.

Floors. The floor is the coolest spot (80° to 100°F/27° to 38°C) in a heated sauna, so you can use almost anything from concrete to tile as a surfacing material.

Three Floor Finishes

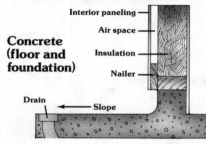

Concrete (floor and foundation)

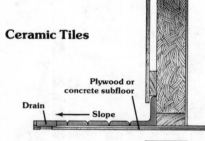

Ceramic Tiles

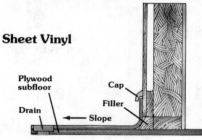

Sheet Vinyl

The best sauna floors are waterproof and slightly sloped toward drains so that water can be used in the sauna during the heat bath and for cleaning. (Water permitted to leak through flooring will eventually cause mildew or dry rot in the wood structure beneath.)

Wooden duckboards (racks of wood strips with spaces between) are often used over concrete floors because they're simple to install, attractive, and easily removed when the sauna needs cleaning. Over a concrete slab, you also can use plastic slats made for sauna use or woven matting that can be removed for periodic cleaning; or you can surface the floor with ceramic tile.

Duckboard Construction

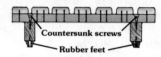

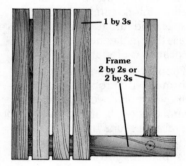

For flooring over a plywood base, you can use ceramic tile, seamless sheet vinyl, or fiberglass. Slope the floor toward a drain, and use only waterproof adhesives during installation.

Though they aren't waterproof, solid wood floors are nonetheless a traditional surfacing material for saunas. Wood is a good insulator and esthetically pleasing, but it also becomes slippery when wet, quickly absorbs perspiration odors, and can be difficult to clean properly. (You should limit the amount of water used in a sauna with a solid wood floor to protect the floor framing from dry rot.)

Indoor-outdoor carpeting is installed in a number of prefabricated saunas, though some sauna experts feel that it has a tendency to trap and breed bacteria.

Framing, Wiring, and Insulation

With your foundation laid you are ready to frame the floor (unless your foundation is a concrete slab), walls, and ceiling; then to wire and insulate.

Framing. If you've poured a slab foundation that will serve as the sauna floor, you can begin framing the walls. If not, you first must construct a subfloor over floor joists that

Framing and Insulation

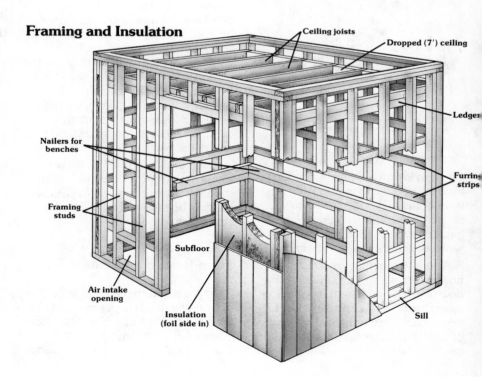

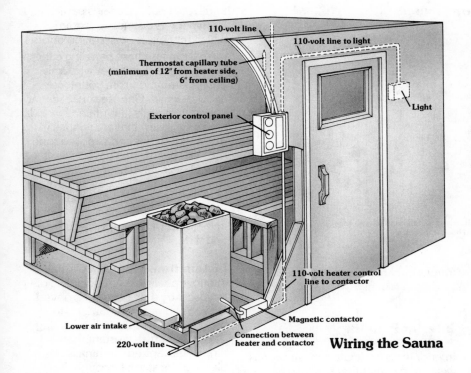

Wiring the Sauna

flow of heat—the higher the rating, the more effective the material. R-value needs vary from region to region (along the mild West Coast, for example, an exterior wall may only need insulation with an R-value of 11; along the East Coast an exterior wall will require at least R-19 insulation). But state and local requirements vary; check with your building department for R-value requirements in your area.

A frequent choice for sauna insulation is foil-faced fiberglass (3½-inch-thick batts usually have an R-value of 11). The batts come in 15″ and 23″ widths with flanges you can staple (do not use glue) to framing studs. The foil side should face in: it creates a partial vapor barrier to prevent moisture from collecting inside the walls, and it reflects some heat back into the sauna.

Doors and Windows

Like the rest of sauna construction, doors and windows must be built to contribute to the sauna's specialized climate. Both must be insulated and properly fitted to the jamb or frame to minimize heat loss.

Doors. When you hang your sauna door, it's important to keep in mind that it will shrink and swell with changes in temperature. If your door doesn't fit just right into the jamb, you may end up either fighting to open it or fighting to keep heat from slipping through the cracks.

Sauna doors measure 6′ to 6′8″ high by 20″ or 24″ wide (the smaller size is better in a small sauna, where heat loss is particularly high every time you open the door). For safety reasons, sauna doors should always

are nailed to the sill (see illustration on page 69 showing platform construction).

When framing the walls, perhaps the easiest technique is to assemble studs, plates, and headers for the door and windows, one section at a time, directly on the slab or subfloor. Each wall section, once assembled, is erected, squared, and nailed to the floor joists through the subfloor, or attached to the concrete slab with anchor bolts or concrete nails.

Rafters, like joists and studs, should be spaced according to code, usually 16″ or 24″ on center.

Wiring. Unless you are an experienced electrician, hire a professional to install the electrical circuits for 1) your stove, control panel, and thermostat, and 2) the lighting. Electrical standards are strict and precise; in a sauna you usually must use wiring that can hold up under 194°F/ 90°C or higher temperatures, and that will withstand moist conditions. You also must locate the wires in dry areas behind the insulation. Check first with your building inspector.

A typical sauna wiring scheme is illustrated above. Note that all switches must go on the outside of the sauna.

Insulation. Good insulation in a sauna keeps heat in and the cost of operating your stove down.

Though spray foams and rigid foam board are sometimes used in prefabricated saunas, they can be difficult to install correctly and may be adversely affected over time by the heat generated inside the sauna.

Your best choice is fiberglass. It comes in long rolls or 4-foot batts and is easy to install. However, always wear gloves, a long-sleeved shirt, loose clothing, and safety glasses when installing fiberglass; stray fibers can cause a surprising amount of irritation to the body.

When selecting insulation, consider the material's "R" rating rather than its thickness. The R-value tells you a material's ability to stop the

The Sauna Door

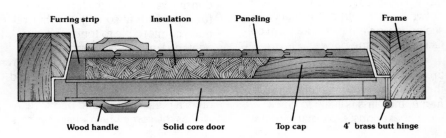

Paneling the Sauna

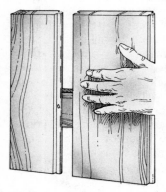

1. **Slide groove of panel over tongue**

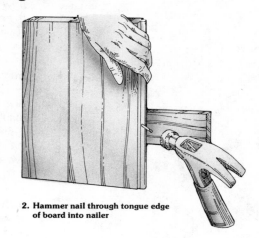

2. **Hammer nail through tongue edge of board into nailer**

open out; they should never be fitted with latching devices that can malfunction and lock you in.

You can either buy prehung doors made specifically for saunas from sauna manufacturers, or you can make your own from a standard solid core door purchased from a supplier that handles custom sizes. (Don't try to build a 6-foot sauna door from a standard 6′8″ solid core door; cutting 8 inches from it to suit the sauna will expose the core to moisture and eventually give you a warped door.) When you do use a solid core door, you need to add a frame, insulation, and paneling.

Sauna doors generally require three hinges (4″ brass spring-loaded butts) to carry their weight; ball bullet or roller catches for latching the door without locking it; and wood handles.

Windows. Even the smallest window will eliminate the claustrophobic feeling you can get in a sauna. Windows, too, let daylight into the room and can give you visual access to a pleasant view.

Whether it's a small square in a door or an entire window wall, your window should be made of thermal glass—double-glazed or double pane tempered glass with air space between. It should be hermetically sealed to prevent moisture from collecting inside the panes.

When you install the glass, make an allowance for it to swell slightly in the heat. If it fits too tightly in the frame, the glass is likely to crack when it expands. Do not use metal

frames or hardware that will become too hot to touch.

Interior Paneling

Interior walls in classic Finnish saunas were simply the other side of exterior walls—rough logs harvested from spruce and pine forests. The logs were dotted with knotholes, and resins yielded a faint woody smell in the heated interior. The hot knotholes and melting resins also sometimes burned bathers.

Interior walls and ceilings in today's custom-built and prefabricated saunas are usually surfaced with unblemished, high-grade woods that are kiln-dried to resist shrinking, cupping, and warping. They are also milled smooth for comfort.

Do not plan to finish the walls and ceiling with any nonwood materials, such as tile, vinyl, fabric, or metals; these materials can become toxic or too hot to touch, or they can constitute a fire hazard. (Using stone, tile, or brick as a fireproof surface near the stove is one exception to this rule.)

Choosing wood. The best woods to use for interior paneling are low-density softwoods which resist heat (dense woods absorb it) and thus remain comfortable to touch in a heated sauna. Such woods include redwood, western red cedar, Alaskan yellow cedar, eastern white pine, and sugar pine. Also included are ponderosa pine, spruce, and hemlock, as well as the somewhat denser cypress

and Douglas fir. (Cedar is particularly known for its distinctive aroma, which minimizes perspiration odors.)

You can purchase paneling either from a sauna distributor who sells precut lumber or from your local lumber dealer. Choose surfaced, vertical grain woods (flat-grained woods tend to splinter) that are relatively free of knotholes and exposed resin pockets; boards that have these flaws should be located near the floor (never on the ceiling), away from bathers. Try to use continuous lengths of wood for paneling to minimize joints that can trap moisture and dirt.

Installation. One way to install interior paneling (sauna builders often use 1 by 4 or 1 by 6 V-grooved tongue and groove boards) is to blind nail it vertically to the framing studs. Using rust-resistant, hot-dipped galvanized finish nails or staples, nail (or staple) through the tongue edge of each board (see illustration above) so the groove of the next panel will hide the nails.

With either tongue and groove or shiplap boards, or their variations, you also can panel horizontally or diagonally, or use a wood pattern of your own design.

Exterior Finishes

Any number of materials—wood shakes or shingles, aluminum, wood or plywood siding, wallboard, face brick, or stone veneer—may be used for the sauna exterior. Your choice will ultimately be determined by your sauna's location, your personal taste and budget, and local building requirements.

As shown in the photographs on pages 58–61, you can adapt a sauna exterior to almost any architectural style. The design can echo the lines and color of your house, or, if you prefer, it can resemble its rustic antecedents in rural Finland.

If you use lumber, you can paint, varnish, or seal it, though it's a good idea to choose a finish that doesn't require frequent reapplication. If the sauna is outdoors, you may prefer to finish it with wood that weathers naturally.